TAX JUSTICE

Social and Moral Aspects of
American Tax Policy

Ronald Pasquariello

UNIVERSITY
PRESS OF
AMERICA

LANHAM • NEW YORK • LONDON

the churches'
CENTER FOR THEOLOGY
AND PUBLIC POLICY

Library of Congress Cataloging in Publication Data

Pasquariello, Ronald D.
  Tax justice.

  "Co-published by arrangement with the Churches' Center
for Theology and Public Policy"—T.p. verso.
  1. Tax incidence—United States. 2. Taxation—United
States. 3. Taxation—United States—Moral and ethical
aspects. I. Churches' Center for Theology and Public
Policy (Washington, D.C.) II. Title.
HJ2322.A3P35   1985   336.2'9   85-3250
ISBN 0-8191-4606-4 (alk. paper)
ISBN 0-8191-4607-2 (pbk. : alk. paper)

Co-published by arrangement with
the Churches' Center for Theology
and Public Policy

For John Mulligan, FMS, who was taxed in many ways during the production of this book.

Acknowledgments

A word of thanks is hardly enough to express the amount of gratitude owed to the friends and colleagues who have participated in various ways in the production of this book. But I want to do at least that, while acknowledging that the wisdom is theirs, any errors mine.

I wish to thank in particular Samantha Sanchez and Floyd Haskell of the Taxpayers Committee for their inspiration and for verifying the technical aspects of this book. Timothy Keating, SM, graciously and conscientiously supplied the research for the sections on tax resistance and on charitable contributions.

Encouragement and enrichment came forth in abundance from the Tax Policy Study Group of the Churches' Center for Theology and Public Policy. Among its most faithful members were Ellen Lynch, CSC, Timothy Keating, SM, Gordon Smith, and Jessica Cannon. Others who participated at various times included Robert Tiller, Mary Cooper, Robert McCan and Woody Ginsburg.

The manuscript, in its various incarnations, had a number of readers. Besides everyone mentioned above, that elite group included Thomas Nuchols and George Ogle.

Finally, this book could not have been possible without the support of the Churches' Center for Theology and Public Policy. Special thanks are due Alan Geyer, its executive director, who encouraged its production when it seemed like the rest of the world was interested in anything but the tax system. Valuable moral support was also forthcoming from Jean Martensen and Robert Cory.

Table of Contents

Introduction

When Jimmy Carter was president, he announced that the tax system was a disgrace. That wasn't really news for most of us. He also said that he intended to do something about it. Well, he didn't, and the tax system remains one of the principal structural sources of social injustice in America.

At the beginning of 1985, new hope for tax change looms. The Treasury Department has taken a bold initiative with its "modified flat tax" proposal. More important than the plan itself is what it signifies: that tax reform has been put on the front burner, where it belongs.

There is also some bad news. Run down the roster of tax reform organizations, and you will find only a handful of public interest tax groups. Most of the tax policy reform groups are organized by businesses and corporations seeking yet another tax exemption. Advocacy organizations representing the interests of the ordinary taxpayer number two or four, depending how one weighs what they are doing. Their budgets are not very large.

This book is a plea to all taxpayers to take a look at the tax system they so often complain about and see to its reform immediately. The book has four purposes: (1) to explain why ethical concerns require tax reform, (2) to lay out some criteria for judging the fairness of the system, (3) to explain the tax system so that interested citizens may better understand it and contribute to the public discussion and to the resolution of the problems, and (4) to demonstrate to Christians that their faith requires them to be concerned about tax reform.

Talk of the complexity of the system seems to scare off potential reformers. True, the system is complex, but so is ballet, or chess, or poker, or football. You need not know all the complexities to understand the game and criticize the procedure. You need not know the intricacies of the system to understand the simple caution to be wary of tax loopholes because they almost always benefit those in the highest tax bracket. Or to understand that the gradual decrease in corporation taxes and the rapid increase in payroll taxes has made the system more and more unfair.

The issues which this book examines are the following: Theological and ethical issues in tax reform, the need for taxation in a democracy, taxation and redistribution of wealth and income, criteria for judging the fairness of the tax system, determining who bears the burden of the system, the declining progressivity of the individual income tax, the erosion of the corporate tax, the increasing regressivity of the payroll tax, and tax expenditures (loopholes)—their identity and how they operate. In the end, it evaluates various proposals for tax reform: the flat tax, loophole closing, the consumption tax, indexing the tax system, wealth taxation, estate and gift taxes. In the appendix there are some suggestions for readers who want to take action.

> *Justice and only justice shall you follow*
> *that you may live and inherit the land*
> *which the Lord your God gives you.*
>
> Deuteronomy 16,20

Chapter 1:
Christians and the Tax System
(On Theological and Ethical Issues in Tax Reform)

The late Stanley Surrey, Assistant Secretary of the Treasury under President Kennedy and tireless pursuer of tax reform, formulated an interesting parable about the tax system. Suppose, the parable goes, a new Secretary of Housing and Urban Development made these proposals to help Americans buy their own homes:

• For a married couple with more than $200,000 in income, the government would pay $50 of every $100 of their mortgage interest costs. The couple would pay the other $50.

• For a married couple with an income of $15,000, the government would pay $22 of every $100 of their mortgage interest costs. This couple would pay the other $78.

• For a married couple earning about $8,000, and too poor to pay any income tax, the government would pay nothing of their mortgage interest costs. This couple would pay the entire interest themselves.[1] Given such a proposal, you would expect the Secretary of Housing to be laughed out of office. Subsidize the rich, while leaving the poor to fend for themselves—something seems out of joint about that idea. It grates against your moral sensibilities and common sense.

Unfortunately, it is not just a parable; it is fact. What has just been described is a tax mechanism that is already in place: the home mortgage interest deduction. This deduction, with which most Americans are very familiar, operates like a government subsidy. By allowing the first couple to deduct 50 percent of its mortgage interest payment, the government is subsidizing them to the tune of $50 per $100 of interest they owe on their mortgage.

Here is how it works for that first couple. With earnings of $200,000, their tax bracket would be 50 percent. For each $100 in mortgage interest they can deduct from their income, they save $50 in taxes. If they can deduct $2,500 mortgage interest in one year, their savings in taxes would be half that or $1,250. The government equivalently gives this rich couple $50 for each $100 they spend on their home mortgage. The average taxpayer, however, receives a benefit of only $22, and the poor nothing at all.

Surrey's parable suggests a number of things about the tax system which will be considered in this book. At this point, we wish to extrapolate those reasons it recommends for Christian involvement with the tax system, tax reform, and tax justice.

In the first place, the parable unmasks a fundamental inequity, namely our system of tax loopholes, of which the mortgage interest deduction is only a small part. On the surface loopholes seem to be available to all taxpayers. Theoretically that is true, but, in reality, they benefit primarily the well-to-do. In our example, the higher a couple's tax bracket, the greater their deduction. The couples with larger incomes could take a proportionally larger deduction, or receive a larger subsidy from the government.

A second reason for Christian concern about the tax system, is this: Through the tax system, the government encourages certain types of economic and social behavior. Whether this is a positive or negative aspect of the system will be discussed in later chapters. That it affects economic and social behavior ought to make Christians sit up and take notice.

The tax system is not a neutral mechanism for raising government revenues, as a growing number of Americans are beginning to realize. The IRS is not just the national bill collector, and the tax system is not the national checking account. Nor is it our national savings account, where we put aside money to pay for our national expenditures. None of these analogies hold because the tax system strongly influences what we do and how we do it. The way it is presently shaped, the tax system is our national scapel, contributing, with the outlay side of the budget, to the shaping of social and economic reality in this country.

The home mortgage interest deduction, for example, encourages people to buy new homes rather than rent homes, or rehabilitate their own homes. This has been a major factor in the development of the suburbs and the decay and decline of the central cities. Looked at from this perspective, it means that the shape of our cities has been influenced by the shape of the tax system. The present condition of cities has affected a whole pattern of economic and social relationships within the country; unemployment, mass movements of peoples to the south and west, the breakdown of the extended family, etc.

The examples are endless. Tax bracket considerations influence workers' decisions about taking a second job or doing overtime work, decisions of the rich about ways to shelter income, business decisions about whether to make long-term or short-term plant improvements, corporate decisions to merge with other companies or to develop better quality products, and so on.

This book is about the federal tax system, but local taxes have similar effect. Our current system of property taxes actually encourages the misuse and abuse of urban land. The current land tax is not just one tax, but two taxes: one on land and the other on improvements on the land. The person who improves the land must pay a higher tax with each improvement. In effect, the one who improves the land by constructing housing, or some other edifice, or submitting it to some profitable use, is penalized. The property tax system encourages owners to leave their land fallow, or not to improve their aging residences, with dire effects on urban life.

These tax-induced judgments shape the economy and the society. They are decisions about the use of our labor, land and capital goods. Put in Christian terms, taxes are one way we exercise our stewardship over our national resources, our own talents and the products we create.

A third reason Surrey's parable suggests to Christians about their involvement in tax reform is this: the tax system is not, as we might believe, redistributive. Tax benefits go to the well-to-do. The system is hardly progressive; it is at best proportional (levying the same rate on all persons), but most likely regressive (putting the burden on the lower and middle-income classes.)

Fourthly, Christians need to be tax-minded in their social action because decisions about taxes affect in particular how this society will treat the poor. In our parable, the poor did not fare so well: They were the only ones who did not receive a subsidy. So also in reality. There is a theoretical top limit (which eludes exact determination) on how much money the government can take from its citizens in taxes. Because of this, if some are exempt from paying taxes, others have to make up the difference. In our present system, it is the well-to-do who can benefit from tax loopholes, exemptions, credits, etc. This means that the others, the lower and middle-income class, have to pay higher taxes than they would were there no exemptions.

Another reason for Christians to become more tax minded: taxes are the revenue side of the federal budget. Taxes constitute the income for those programs that this society has determined are needed to operate essential services and to terminate the terrible consequences of poverty in this country. A system which unnecessarily exempts those who can afford to pay their fair share means a diminished capability to meet the requirements of those programs, of the American instinct for fair play, and the Christian concern for justice. What is involved here is not insignificant. Tax exemptions amount to billions of dollars, $365 billion in 1985. This means that we exempted about 40 percent of the amount needed to meet our budgetary expenses that year, and, of course, much more than that year's enormous $200 billion federal deficit.

The preceding list of reasons for Christian involvement in the tax system points in two theological directions: One has to do with the role of humans in God's creation: the other has to do with the important issue of social justice. They are examined in the next two sections.

Creation's Mandate and the Tax System

It is certainly made clear at the very beginning of the Bible that our task as humans is to shape economic and social reality. If this is true and if the tax system is one of the levers that does so, than Christians should be participating in its design and assuring that it reflects the values that Christianity wants to see incarnated in society.

The mandate comes from Genesis: "Then God said, 'And now we will make human beings; they will be like us and resemble us. They will have power over the fish, the birds, and all animals, domestic and wild, large and small'. So God created human beings, making them to be like himself." (Gen. 1, 26-27). The text tells us something about ourselves, as it reveals something about God. About God it tells us that the Creator God is a collaborating God. About us, it says that we are images of this creative, collaborative God.

What does it mean to be the image of this God? It means to be creators at the behest of the Creator God, to be responsible for the creation, along with the biblical God, who not only creates it, but continuously intervenes to save it. We are to respond to the call of God at work in history to shape the world in light of its future, the coming kingdom.

To say that we are responsible for the creation is to say that we are to be shapers of the world, negotiators of it in its movement towards the future that God has planned for it. That future is of course the kingdom of freedom, peace, love, justice, mutuality. To be collaborative, creative shapers of the world means that we must be involved with it, assuring that the values of freedom, peace, love, justice, sustainability, participation and others are incarnated in the world in anticipation of the arrival of the kingdom.

The lesson of Genesis is this: To be human, to be made in the image of the Creator, is to be endowed with the ability to give shape to the world, to have the ability to participate fully in one's society, to have one's voice heard, to make a difference. To be human is to have the mandate and the power to shape things. Called to be God's collaborative agents, we share a common mission to move beyond where we are at any given time, to move in the direction of the coming kingdom, if we are going to be true to ourselves. Responsible action with regard to the world is devotion to God: It is service. This world is God's world and God, the Bible tells us, has chosen to achieve his/her will in collaboration with us.

If this is what we are to be, shapers of the economic and social reality of the world, and if indeed this is what the tax system does, then we must be involved with the tax system as a Christian duty. All the more so because the tax system is one of our creations. We have designed it; we have amended it; we have shaped it. Whatever distortions it contains of essentially Christian values, are the product of our intention or of our indifference. In either case, we have a responsibility, by virtue of the fact that we are images of God, or by virtue of the fact that we are responsible for the impact of the products of our own hands, to assure that the tax system helps deliver a just, sustainable and participatory world.

Justice and Creation's Mandate

Implicit in the biblical charge for humans to shape the world towards the coming kingdom is the biblical mandate to act justly. The Christian work of shaping creation must be a work of justice. Working together with God to shape the world towards the coming kingdom is a work of justice. We are not just building up the world, but building a just society, a harmonious creation.

These themes come together poignantly in Psalm 72, which gives a biblical understanding of the role of government by describing the ideal king: "He shall be like rain coming down on the meadow, like showers watering the earth. Justice shall flower in his days, and profound peace, till the moon be no more." (Ps. 72, 6-7)

The psalm does not leave any doubt about the meaning of justice and peace: "For he shall rescue the poor man when he cries out, and the afflicted when he has no one to help him. He shall have pity for the lowly and the poor; the lives of the poor he shall save. From fraud and violence he shall redeem them, and precious shall their blood be in his sight." (Ps. 72, 13-15)

The connection is clear. The whole of reality is directed in the Bible towards the coming kingdom of peace, justice and love. The work of creation is to shape the world towards that future. The work of creation is the work of justice. The necessity to be just arises out of the mandate to be images of God, because the biblical God is the God of justice.

Israel's understanding of creation is a product of her experience of the God of the Exodus. The God who saves is the God who creates. Exodus is just one aspect of God's salvific work for the whole world which the divine one has directed towards consummation in the kingdom of peace, justice and love.

At the heart of Christian stewardship is the God of justice, Who claims, through the prophet Jeremiah, to be known only in the doing of justice. Jeremiah says to King Jehoahaz: "Must you prove your rank among kings by competing with them in cedar? Did not your father eat and drink. He did what was right and just, and it went well with him. Because he dispensed justice to the weak and poor, it went well with him. Is this not true knowledge of me? says the Lord." (Jer. 22, 15-17). We cannot be indifferent to injustice because where there is injustice, our stewardship is in question.

We often define distributive justice as giving each person his/her due. Christians need to be dissatisfied with that definition as insufficient to the creative intentions of God. Distributive justice presupposes not only the right of individuals to the goods given by creation, but it also presupposes the right that persons have to participate in the creation of a society in which justice, love, peace and mutuality are effective, a society which is characterized by communal well-being and mutual interdependence. These goods are not individual and private, but essentially public and social. In a creationist perspective, distributive justice seeks to establish a society in which persons are interdependently centers of power engaged in the creation of social and political structures that make participation in the common good a reality. This kind of collaborative justice cannot be realized in situations of drastic economic or social inequality.

Principles of Justice and Taxation

This perspective on distributive justice leads to some principles which establish a context within which to consider the tax system.[2]

1. Social justice requires a society to equitably share the benefits from social collaboration. Social collaboration is fundamental to any society. Without it, the society could not maintain itself. There are benefits that come from that collaboration and it is these benefits that this principle addresses.

These benefits are not just the sum of the individual contributions. In addition to that it is necessary to take into account a synergistic effect, an effect that results from the collectivity formed when numbers of individuals interact collaboratively.

William Ryan[3] offers a hypothetical example. Suppose 20 persons working together produce 200 eggbeaters a day; and that the same 20 working separately produce 5 each, or 100 a day. The 100 additional egg-beaters produced by the collaborating workers are a result of the collectivity that exists when they work together—collaborate—rather than working as solitary individuals.

The principle stated above suggests that those extra hundred eggbeaters belong not to any one individual, but to the collectivity of 20 workers. But actually those eggbeaters are the product of a broader social collaboration: Those who invented the eggbeater and designed its components, those who produced the physical material, those who developed the production process, etc. In addition, as Ryan points out,[4] the value of the eggbeater depends on the existence of eggs and on the complicated process by which eggs arrive at the dining room table in the form of an omelet or angel food cake.

When we consider more complicated processes of production—automobiles, houses, interstate highway systems, computers, international trade—the role of the individual diminishes and the function of social collaboration looms larger.

One final point: this principle talks about "sharing" rather than "distributing." It moves in the direction of understanding "distributive" justice as "collaborative" or "participatory" justice. Besides coordinating with the idea of the justice described earlier in this chapter, this conception of justice responds to the criticism of distributive justice that understands it to mean the literal dividing of the goods and benefits equally among all persons as one would divide a pie. Not all society's goods can be so divided. Fairness indeed demands an appropriate distribution throughout society of sufficient means for sustaining life and preserving liberty.

Sharing, in addition, stresses the right of access to those goods which cannot be so divided but which are the necessary conditions for full participation in the shaping society. Among the resources we share—i.e., which cannot be divided and parcelled out—are, obviously, public parks, beaches, libraries, sewer systems, water systems, etc. Still more important public goods that are shared and ultimately redound to the benefit of the society as well as individuals are education, government, pollution control, and yes, national defense.

This principle addresses a popular notion that each person is entitled to whatever reward he/she is able to obtain from his/her natural abilities. In this view, the assumption is that whatever results from these abilities is necessarily just, and that the needs of the poor are to be left to charity.

The principle enunciated here takes a different position. It says that the society has a moral claim on all income and wealth at least to the extent that income or wealth was obtained from social interactions and the opportunities and resources the society possesses.

2. Social justice requires that the major social institutions be justly designed.

These institutions include legislative, legal, market, health, budgetary, tax and other systems for the distribution of goods and services. Too often we overlook the social impact of these and other institutions. We fail to recognize that these institutions, by virtue of the very way they are organized and by the power they wield in the society, shape our lives. Think of what would happen were we to dissolve, for example, the banking system or the transportation system. Our whole way of interacting would change suddenly and dramatically.

It was Marshal McLuhan who zeroed in on the importance of the design of contemporary systems over the content the systems produced. His slogan was "the medium is the message." His own pun on that slogan, "the medium is the massage," is more explicit. His point: systems massage us. The way a system is designed has a great, if not greater, influence on us than the product it produces.

In our present set up, the tax system is one of the major social institution for achieving social justice. Many of the other systems are dependent on it for their own operation, but not necessarily for their ultimate effectiveness.

Tax reform too-often means making internal adjustments to the system by changing particular statutes. And too often this has meant instituting yet another tax loophole. The effect of these adjustments has been a distortion of the system as a whole, so that the system itself has become not just a jungle of injustices, but an unjust structure.

Justice is not just a matter of assuring that individual statutes, laws or regulations achieve just results, but it is a question of the design of the system itself. Is the system so designed that its impact is equitably distributed? Does it reach all taxpayers fairly? Does it touch all appropriate forms of benefits that accrue to individuals from cooperative interaction? Is it sufficiently effective for helping us meet our national priorities? Does it have a desirable impact on the society and economy? Does it recognize differences in ability-to-pay?

Justice in the design of our social institutions is as important as justice in the allocation or distribution of our national resources. Justice can only be expected when our social institutions are justly designed. A poorly or unjustly designed social institution cannot bear just fruit.

3. *The tax system must be so designed that it contributes to making the after-tax shares of income and wealth equitable.*

The third principle has to do with the effect of our social institutions as mediating structures between the society and the individual. It simply says that if the before-tax distribution of shares of income and wealth in society are not enough to satisfy the demands of distributive and collaborative justice, than the tax system ought to be one of the mechanisms used by the society to make the after-tax shares equitable.

This principle ought to be understood broadly, because redistribution occurs in a number of places in the society. To address the issue of redistribution satisfactorily requires examining the structure of the entire public order, i.e., all of the major social institutions. From a public policy perspective, the tax system, along with the outlay side of the budget it funds, are the principal systems for meeting our defined redistribution needs. And the tax system should be designed to meet these needs.

4. *The tax system must be so arranged, in concert with other systems of disbution, that the least advantaged receive the greatest benefit.*

This principle merely puts the tax system within the context of the biblical option for the poor. The principle gets to the heart of the matter. A person's income is a product of individual talent (sometimes; much income is the result of inheritance or chance) and the social cooperation that constitutes our society. To the extent that this income is a social product, to that extent has the society a moral claim on it. A person's income is just only to the extent that the goods of the society are equitably shared or distributed. Where the distribution is inequitable, the poor have a moral claim on the portion of national income needed to justify the situation.

Rendering to Caesar . . .

Books have been written about the meaning of this statement that the New Testament attributes to Jesus: "Render to Caesar that things that are Caesar's and to God the things that are God's" (Lk 20,25). The text is used in different constellations of contexts that deal with the relationship of Christianity to the State. Here, the focus is on what it has to say about Christians and taxes.

The text is important. Since it is identical in Matthew, Mark and Luke, it is probably an authentic pronouncement of Jesus. The numerous interpretations of the text seem to fall into two groups.[5] The majority of scholars believe that Jesus was advocating support for the Roman order. They differ, however, over how strongly he affirmed this support in comparison with his emphasis on the things of God. For them Jesus is stating that we have two parallel sets of obligation, one to God and one to the state, and both are to be met. A minority of scholars, Brandon and Kennard foremost among them, maintain that Jesus opposes the payment of taxes altogether.[6] Significantly for the theological perspective emphasized here, some scholars among the majority have picked up the "image" resonances in the text as suggested in Jesus' question about the coin of tribute: "Whose image is on it?" Giblin agrees with them, asserting that the "things of God" are humans, who in a biblical setting, are the images of God in contrast with the image on the coin. Rendering to God means that humans are to offer themselves to the Lord or repay him with their service, "inasmuch as they bear his image and are inscribed with his name."[7] Jesus did not submit himself to the question posed to him. Instead he pounded home his essential message: that the fundamental duty of all is to serve the Lord.

Cassidy, agreeing with Giblin, suggests we have to view the text contextually, that is in concert with other reports the evangelists give about Jesus' approach to the Roman social and political order.[8] The evangelists always have the priority of the divine order over the human order in mind. The only areas, therefore in which Caesar can expect allegiance are those in which his patterns are in conformity with God's desired patterns.

For our text, this means: God must be rendered to even if to do so requires a rejection of political patterns which are contrary to God's desired patterns. The social policies and practices of the nation are to be evaluated and responded to from the standpoint of the social patterns God desires. For Cassidy, and for us, the social patterns are primarily service and the option for the poor. The text comes out strongly for these two, particularly in light of the fact that the "things of God" are humans made in God's image. Caesar is to be rendered to where political patterns conform to these divine intentions.

Conclusion

This chapter offers a rationale for participation by Christians in the shaping of the tax system. Wherever social and economic reality is being shaped to the weal or woe of humans, they—humans, but especially

Christians—as images of the collaborating God, are required to participate in that process. And the tax system, as presently structured, has that effect.

Distributive justice needs to be understood broadly as productive, collaborative justice, in the active sense of establishing the conditions in which persons can realize the potential of the promises of creation.

Among the justice principles that are operative here are the following:

1. Social justice requires a society to equitably share the advantages of social cooperation.

2. Social justice requires that the major social institutions be justly designed.

3. The tax system must be so designed that it contributes to making the after-tax shares of income and wealth equitable.

4. The tax system must be so arranged, in concert with other systems of distribution, that the least advantaged receive the greatest benefit.

Finally, the text about "rendering to Caesar . . . " reminds all Christians that the demands of the state are to be seen within the context of the intentions of God for the world.

A Note on Tax Resistance

What we commonly call tax resistance or tax refusal is described as tax protest by the Internal Revenue Service and by tax law. As a question of law, it has been around almost from the beginning of the Internal Revenue Code. Resisters have withheld their taxes for religious reasons like pacifism, and such political ones as disenchantment with the Federal Reserve System.

There were tax resisters in second century Egypt. Resistance to war through tax refusal appears to date back to the opposition of Danish peasants to the war against Sweden in 1515. The persistent conflict between English Kings and their nobility over wars and taxes stretches across the whole history of medieval England.

Until recently, only the traditional peace Churches (the Quakers, the Mennonites, and the Church of the Brethren) have been known for tax resistance in the United States. The Quakers and Mennonites resisted war taxes throughout the eighteenth century. Some Quakers were disowned by their religious communities for paying taxes for the Revolutionary War.[9]

Henry David Thoreau, the most famous non-religious war tax protester and guru of the present movement, was imprisoned for refusing to pay taxes for the Mexican War. The Boston Tea Party and the Whiskey Rebellion, out of which our nation was born, were secular protests over taxes.

The dawn of the nuclear age has qualitatively changed the stakes of the war game. It has given tax resistance, once thought the preserve of dreamy idealists, widespread respectability. Humans now have the technology to engineer their own destruction. What is at stake is the fate of the earth and the entire human race. "Limited nuclear war" is simply not possible. As one of the characters in the film, "The Day After," said when reflecting on the power of nuclear bombs: "There is no nowhere anymore." The world is held hostage to certain superpowers, and, more to the point, to certain elites within those superpowers.

IRS Commissioner Roscoe Egger said in a speech to the American Bar Association that he was able to identify 6,600 protesters in 1978. Two years later that number had more than doubled to 15,285[10] and it seems to be growing still as a result of the nuclear freeze movement.

Roman Catholic Archbishop Raymond G. Hunthausen of Seattle is the most recent striking example of tax resistance. He announced in 1981 that he had refused to pay 50 percent of his taxes to the federal government. Fifty percent is what he estimates is the portion of individual's taxes due to military expenditures and the debt from past wars. He has deposited the withheld money in a fund to be used for charitable peaceful purposes. His rationale for this action is biblically based, though it has ultimately to do with the sacredness of human life: "Our tax dollars are our freely offered incense to a nuclear idol which scientists and physicians tell us may destroy life on earth. You and I, friends, are paying for that crucifixion, at least until we become tax resisters to our nuclear idol."[11]

There have been numerous public witnesses of Christians who contend that it is a violation of their conscience to fund with their tax payments an armaments policy that violates the Gospel as they understand it. Pacifism and tax resistance are certainly valid responses to the Gospel. It is not clear, however, that the gospels place an absolute mandate upon the shoulders of Christians to take this kind of action. There has been a wide divergence of opinion on the matter within the Christian tradition. It is, as Hunthausen has made clear, an imperative that one can arrive at only after careful and prayerful reflection. There are, after all, other means Christians can take, on the basis of their understanding of the Gospel, to achieve the same ends.

From a legal standpoint, the argument touches upon the first amendment rights to freedom of religion which substantiate the conscientious objector status. Do they also substantiate conscientious objection to the use of tax revenue to fund military projects that the taxpayer cannot conscientiously condone? This type of tax resistance is, at present, illegal. Congressman Ronald Dellums of California, along with two dozen others, has sponsored a World Peace Tax Fund Bill in every session of Congress since 1972. It would allow payment of a portion of one's taxes equal to a proportionate share of military expenditures to a government trust fund that would support such services as a   National   Peace Academy, disarmament efforts, international exchanges, and other peace related programs.

Refusing to comply with the tax code by withholding taxes is a high risk, serious offense for which prosecution should generally be presumed. The IRS has shown itself to be rather selective in the prosecution of tax protesters. It is an uncomfortable, conspicuously public issue with which IRS would rather not deal. The longest sentence for tax protest seems to have been about nine months in federal prison.

[1]This example is taken from *Tax Politics.* Robert M. Brandon, Jonathan Rowe, and Thomas H. Stanton (New York: Pantheon Books, 1976), pp. 38-39.

[2]These principles are based in part on ideas from John Rawls, *A Theory of Justice* (Cambridge, MA: Harvard University Press, 1971). See also Charles R. O'Kelley, Jr. "Rawls, Justice, and the Income Tax," *Georgia Law Review,* 16 (Fall, 1981), pp. 1-32.

[3]William Ryan, *Equality* (New York: Pantheon Books, 1981), p. 54.

[4]Ryan, pp. 54-55.

[5]See H. Giblin, " 'The Things of God' in the Question Concerning Tribute to Caesar," *Catholic Biblical Quarterly,* 33(1971), pp. 510-514.

[6]Richard J. Cassidy, *Jesus, Politics, and Society: A Study of Luke's Gospel.* (Maryknoll, NY: Orbis Books, 1978), p. 56.

[7]Giblin, p. 525.

[8]Cassidy, p. 56.

[9]A brief account of the history of tax resistance can be found in Bill Samuel, "Refusing War Taxes," *The Catholic Worker* (December, 1982), pp. 7-8.

[10]Karl Meyer, "The Practical Side of Tax Resistance," *National Catholic Reporter* (Feb. 5, 1982), p. 7.

[11]Archbishop Raymond Hunthausen, "Our Nuclear War Preparations Are the Global Crucifixion of Jesus," *National Catholic Reporter* (February 12, 1982), p. 1.

Taxes are what we pay for civilized society.

Oliver Wendell Holmes, Jr.

Chapter 2:
Is It Fair to Pay Taxes?
(On the Social Uses of Taxes)

The birth trauma that spawned the union of the thirteen colonies was a tax revolt. British attempts to tax the Americans in the Sugar Act of 1764 and the Stamp Act of 1765 resulted in swift protests from the colonies, the eloquent slogan that "taxation without representation is tyranny," and of course the Revolutionary War.

Just how large was this tax burden that precipitated the revolt? Historian R.R. Palmer has calculated that the British paid about the highest per capita taxes among Europeans—26 English shillings in 1765. In the same year, the tax burden in the six American colonies was about one shilling! These Colonialists had the lightest tax burden of any people of the western world except the Poles.[1] American taxes are still not high in comparison to other Western industrial nations, though resistance to taxation has become an American tradition—as the Propositions 13, and 2 1/2, the TRIM Amendments and the like testify. It is part of the cultural context that forms our thinking about government and life in these United States. Taxation, with or without representation, is unpopular among Americans.

Distaste for taxation is as old as taxation itself. Witness this New Testament attitude: "The Pharisee stood and prayed thus with himself, 'God, I thank thee that I am not like other men, extortioners, unjust, adulterers, or even like this tax collector'." (Luke 18,11). Similar statements were probably scratched on cave walls in the Neolithic Age.

There is a tendency among those who attempt to justify taxation to say that it is merely a necessary evil. Anyone who would go beyond that could risk being pommeled off stage. Being at a safe distance from the reader, let me claim: taxation is essentially good. And let me quickly defend myself by stressing that I said taxation, not taxes. Some are unbearable and too many are unjust. But the idea of taxation itself is neither.

To understand this apparent foray into the fine art of hair splitting, one needs to reflect on the necessity of government. Government is fundamentally the way humans group together to guarantee their existence into the future. Without this cooperative association, individual humans could hardly maintain their existence. Humans would have long ago lost out to the ravages of the elements, natural or human. Government is essentially good, and the means needed to support it—taxation among other things—are essentially good. The corporate center of our social organization could not be maintained without the necessary financial support.

The government is often taken to task for what it takes away in taxes. Strangely, it is most often taken to the woodshed for this by the men who are running for its highest office, namely, the presidential candidates. But taxes pay for public goods we buy collectively. The goods they buy are good investments: bridges, highways, education, health, housing, national defense. And all of this has an economic spinoff. Government spending contributes to economic growth. It increases demand, generates jobs, facilitates business interactions, augments the productive capacity of the population, links cities and townships.

Within government, it is the federal budget that takes the heat for government expenditures. It is the whipping boy for those who bemoan the growth of government. Yet in actuality, only a small portion of the budget stays with the government. What the budget really reveals about the government is that its main activity is check writing. For example, as proposed by President Reagan for fiscal year 1984:

• 42 percent of the budget would take the form of direct payments to individuals (including social security, medicare, unemployment, federal retirement programs, food stamps and welfare)

• 29 percent would go to national defense (military hardware, research and development, salaries, maintenance of military installations)

• 12 percent would pay interest on national debt

• 11 percent would go to state and local governments (highway aid, sewage treatment, medicaid, community development, housing, education)

Only about 6 percent is left after all these commitments are taken care of. It is this relatively small percentage which is used to pay for all other federal operations. This amount is what the berated federal bureaucracy consumes.

The tax dollar is not a bad investment. While one cannot expect government to run like a business—because elected officials need to be responsible to voters not profits—still it is sobering to realize that most businesses run hugely higher overhead costs.

Is 6 percent too high? Contrary to the impression given by some presidential candidates and some political ideologues, there does not seem to be a magic number for the federal government share in the economy beyond which one dare not go. Comparisons across countries show that there is no obvious relation between economic performance and the government share in the economy. Countries whose governments have grown more rapidly have also shown better economic performance.

The federal budget has grown rapidly in the past couple of decades, because the engine of expenditures is being driven by the growth of the population and consequent increasing demands on government, not by decisions to "spend, spend, spend." Because of the way the budget breaks down—with about one-fifth of the total for social security, and other payments for unemployment, medicare and medicaid and for federal retirement programs—population growth increases the size of our national expenditures.

How the Federal Dollar Is Spent

A quick glance at the outlay side of the federal budget gives a fair picture of what the federal funds are spent on. The chart on the next page pictures President Reagan's 1984 budget proposal, the budget he sent to Congress in January, 1983.

These administration figures need one slight adjustment to give the reader an accurate picture of how government dollars are spent. There are some military expenses hidden among the non-military portions of the pie graph. One of these is obvious. It is the 3 percent allotted to veteran benefits and services, which, while they include health services and retirement benefits, are expenditures that are the result of war. Another outlay due to past wars is a large portion of the national debt. It has been conservatively estimated at 61.8 percent of the national debt.

Taking these two factors into consideration, military spending constitutes about 40 percent of the federal budget.[2]

"Assistance to the poor," which amounts to only five cents out of every federal dollar, includes food stamps, child nutrition, Supplemental Security Income, Aid to Families with Dependent Children (Welfare), the earned income tax credit, refugee assistance, low-income energy assistance, subsidized housing and other housing assistance, and other smaller programs.

The issue of the impact of the federal budget on the well-being of the poor merits special consideration, particularly in a book that purports to look at the budget from a biblical perspective. However, a brief interlude on how budgetary expenditures are determined is necessary to give the reader an idea of how decisions are made to spend our tax dollars.

FY 1984 Budget Outlays

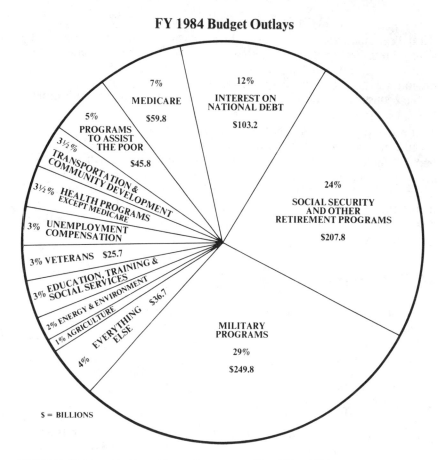

SOURCE: *Budget of the United States Government, Fiscal Year 1984*

How Federal Expenditures Are Decided On

Congress, not the President, controls the national purse strings. This is because Congress, according to the Constitution has the "power of the purse." In practice, however, the President proposes and Congress disposes. Each year, the President sends a fully detailed budget proposal to Capitol Hill for congressional approval. Most often the President gets what he wants. Even presidents who had to deal with hostile congresses have done well. Historically, Congress has stayed within a ten percent range of the President's requests.

In order to come to its final decision, Congress each year follows a strict, but malleable timetable called the budget process. The process requires that Congress make specific financial decisions by specific deadlines, to assure that the nation has a budget by the beginning of each fiscal year.[3]

Congress and the President are the principal actors in formulating the annual budget. There are however other actors who have a great deal of influence.

Inconspicuous, but omnipresent, are the organized lobbyists. Most represent oil interests, tobacco interests, dairy interests, the unions, the housing industry and so on. They lobby for favorable tax legislation as well as for and against pertinent (for them) federal outlays and regulations. Noncommercial lobbys (the National Low Income Housing Coalition, for example, NETWORK, the Coalition for a New Foreign and Military Policy, the Children's Defense Fund, the members of Interfaith Action for Economic Justice, and of the Washington Interfaith Staff Committee) are also present and effective, though they represent a much smaller segment of the organized lobbys.

Two other less tangible actors which influence the federal budget are "the public mood" and "social and economic conditions."

Since a major concern of politicians is serving their constituents, their perception of what these constituents want often colors their decisions. Sometimes this perception of the "public mood" is more persuasive than the reality. President Reagan won most of his economic proposals in 1981 because many lawmakers believed that the country was behind him. Survey data indicated otherwise. While many Americans wanted increased military spending, they also wanted increased, not diminished, social spending. Despite the facts, the public mood was perceived to be conservative and militaristic, and that perception won the day.

"Social and economic conditions" consist mainly of projections concerning the direction of unemployment and inflation. Most of the federal budget is devised on the basis of projections of what the rates of inflation and unemployment will be. Projections of the rate of inflation, for example, help lawmakers decide on how much money needs to be put into poverty programs that are affected by the prices of food, medical care, shelter, or the probable cost of interest on the national debt. The projected rate of unemployment indicates how many persons will most likely take advantage of unemployment compensation, or fall below the poverty level and become new clients for the poverty programs. Both of these factors, unemployment and inflation, help determine the size of the stimulus that the economy needs to continue to grow.

The Total Amount Government Spends

The dollar amounts that make up the federal budget are so large that they strain our ability to comprehend their significance. Congressman James Jones offered this metaphor for 1.5 trillion dollars (the cost of military spending from 1981-1986). He said that if one were to have spent one million dollars each day since the birth of Jesus Christ, one would have disposed of only half that sum.

For a clear idea of the dollar amounts that are at stake in the tax system, it helps to have some perspective on the total amount government spends. Two comparisons may be helpful: the amount the federal government spends as a percentage of the Gross National Product; and the total amount the federal government spends in comparison to other industrial nations.

1. Federal Finances and the Gross National Product.

The Gross National Product (GNP) is the total sales value of the goods and services produced by the nation. In a very broad sense, it is how much it would cost an individual who wanted to buy all the goods and services the nation produced. Recalculated each year, it consists of consumer goods and investment goods, and is a measure of the value of the economy as a whole, i.e., of the economic wealth of the nation.

A key question for economists and federal policy makers is the portion of GNP that is attributable to the federal government. By measuring federal budgetary outlays as a portion or percentage of the GNP, we get an idea of the significance of total federal spending. In 1965, for example, federal finances amounted to 18 percent of the GNP.[4] For the ten years before Reagan became President they averaged 21.3 percent. The budget was 23 percent of the GNP when Reagan took office in fiscal year 1981. Two years later, federal spending in fiscal year 1983 was 25.2 percent of the GNP—meaning that one-fourth of our national wealth was being used by the government in various ways. This was the highest percentage since World War II.

When used as a gauge of the size of government, as some politicians and economists use them, these figures can be disturbing. What they actually reveal, however, is something about the role of the federal government in the economy.

The difference has to do with the way transfer payments are figured in. Transfer payments include social security payments, unemployment compensation, help for the disabled or disadvantaged, plus subsidies of various kinds. These payments are not part of the GNP, though they have grown tremendously as part of the federal budget. They are not part of it because they are made for social purposes, not in payment to a person for a useful service. No production takes place in exchange for a transfer payment. Food stamps, for example, are transfer payments. The recipient does not produce anything either in goods or services to earn them. They are given to the poor person on the understanding that she/he cannot otherwise afford to buy food. Transfer payments came to $280 billion dollars in 1981—42.6 percent of the federal budget for that year.

Upon careful analysis, it becomes apparent that real growth in government, as measured against the GNP, has been in terms of transfer payments.[5] The federal government buys virtually the same fraction of goods and services from the economy as it did in 1949. Transfer payments, however, are up tenfold since 1929. This means that, despite the cry of an expanding federal government, the federal government grew slowly, and almost entirely in response to population growth. War, unfortunately, has also been a contributing factor. Aside from transfer payments, most of the federal purchasing of GNP has to do with warfare. In 1981, for example, almost two thirds of the federal share of GNP (using the formulas given in the preceding section and correcting for transfer payments) was for military purposes. Among the things we are paying for on the installment plan are past wars.

2. The Total Amount Government Spends in Relation to Other Industrialized Countries.

Some specialists fall into the trap of seeing all reality from the particular perspective of their speciality. A behaviorist, for example, may decide that the whole of reality can be explained in terms of stimulus and response, and disregard evidence to the contrary. The problem: his/her speciality looms so large and becomes so totally involving that he/she cannot see beyond it. It becomes his/her "world" in a sense.

When citizens look at their government finances, they tend to do the same thing. They measure its size by the numbers they are confronted with, in comparison perhaps to their own budget, or their own sense of what a lot of money is. However, when our own national finances are compared to other similar countries, they take on a new perspective.

It may surprise the reader to learn that most countries whose economies grew faster than ours and had superior economic performance over recent decades spend more, not less, than we do on domestic social programs. The Congressional Budget Office (CBO) reports that in every European country whose economy grew faster than ours from 1960-1980, government expenditures constitute a substantially larger portion of the gross domestic product than in the U.S. The CBO flatly states that there seems to be no relationship between having a smaller proportion of the economy devoted to government expenditures and achieving better economic performance (a matter to be taken up in chapter nine).

In addition, CBO found that most countries whose economies have grown faster than ours also have larger budget deficits than we do. CBO concluded that "the degree of a country's success in achieving economic growth is not directly related to the existence or magnitude of its public sector deficits."[6] The significance of this is astounding: it means that growth with equity is possible. Most of those countries with economic growth superior to ours in recent decades have also provided more government services to their citizens than we have.

In conclusion, this survey of the scope of federal spending suggests that it is not as large as it would appear to be, and that social spending is not necessarily an impediment to economic growth.

Government Expenditures for the Poor and the Rich

There is no doubt that poverty is rising in America.[7] Over two million people were added to the poverty roles in 1981, and four million more people the following year. Nearly 35 million Americans lived below the poverty level in 1983—15.2 percent of the population, the highest rate since 1965. This means that one out of every seven persons in the richest country in the world is classified among the poor.

The tragedy is that poverty had declined to 11.9 percent of the population by 1979.

Tragic too is the face of poverty in America. It is more likely to be the face of a woman or child and white, black or Hispanic. In 1982:

• Families headed by a single woman with no male in the household had a poverty rate of 36.6 percent.

• 21.3 percent—13.1 million—of the nation's children were among the poor

• 35.6 percent of the Blacks—who made up only 12 percent of the total population—were poor.

• 29 percent of Hispanics were among the nation's poor

• 14.6 percent of the elderly were poor

This kind of poverty among the weakest members of the society is deplorable, but even more tragic is the myth that we are doing well by the poor, that we are helping them as best we can.

Other countries do better for their citizens than we do. A close look at the status of the major poverty programs in 1984 indicates our national lack of generosity.[8]

Between 1980 and 1984 decreases in federal welfare spending and increases in real tax burdens for low income working families caused substantial reductions in the real disposable income of poor families. Unless families were able to increase their real wages by extremely large amounts, their standards of living declined. For example:

• The disposable income of a family of three with earnings at or near the poverty level fell from $9,665 in 1980 to $8,508 in 1984. This is a real decline of 12 percent.

• Families with earnings at one-half the poverty level experienced a real decline in income of 18.7 percent. To maintain its income at 1980 levels, a family would have needed about 72 percent wage increase in 1984.

The principal causes of these income losses were reductions in AFDC and food stamps and increases in real tax burdens for low income families:

• From 1980-1983, benefits for these programs and other means-tested programs dropped 15.5 percent for each poor person in the United States.

• In 1980, a mother and two children with gross earnings at half the poverty level qualified for AFDC benefits in 46 states; in 1984 they could receive benefits in only 24 states.

• From 1980 to 1984, federal tax burdens for families at or below poverty tripled, while taxes for most of the rest of the population stayed the same or declined.

Our national tendency to cluster all human service government programs under the heading of "social programs" contributes to the false perception of our generosity to the poor. Programs to help the impoverished do not make up a very big part of the federal budget. There are two types of social programs which provide benefits and services: the entitlement programs, which are available to certain categories of persons without regard to their income (among them: social security, medicare and other pension programs), and the means-tested programs, which are limited to persons with insubstantial incomes.

The people who fall into these two categories have very different income profiles. About 85 percent of those in the first category have incomes above the poverty line, and, among recipients of civil service or military pensions, the percentage above the poverty line is still higher. By contrast, nearly half of the food stamp households have gross incomes below $300 a

month, and over 90 percent are below the poverty line during the period
they receive stamps.

While close to 50 percent of the budget as a whole is devoted to entitlement and benefit programs, only about 10 percent is devoted to the basic
programs that are targeted on the lower income groups (food stamps,
AFDC, SSI, medicaid, free and reduced price school meals; supplemental
nutrition programs for low income pregnant women, infants and children,
etc.) The budget for social security is more than twice the total budgeted for
all low income programs combined.[9]

Modestly put, our perception of government generosity to the poor is
much greater than the reality. And the situation does not improve when
one takes the tax side of the budget into consideration. For example, when
tax breaks for insurance and medical payments are taken into account, the
government spends as much on health care for the rich as it does for the
poor. Per capita health care expenditures are larger for the poor, who are a
smaller part of the population, but "overall, the government spends about
the same on the poor and near-poor as it does on the middle-income and
high income population," according to a study by the National Center for
Health Services Research.[10] There is more to be said about how the tax
system favors the rich. That discussion is taken up in chapter five.

Budget Deficits

Given a budget deficit, there are three ways in which it can be paid for.
One way is for the government to print and distribute more money
(increase the money supply). Another is for the government to sell bonds to
the public. Or, the government can raise taxes. Americans need to know
something about deficits, because of their impact on taxes, if not for the
fact that poll after poll indicates deficits are high among their major public
policy concerns.

A deficit results any year the government spends more than it takes in
taxes. Thus in Ronald Reagan's proposed 1984 budget, he planned to spend
$805.9 billion, while intending to take in only $723.0 billion in taxes. The
difference, $97.2 billion, would be the projected deficit for 1984.

To cover the deficit, the government borrows from the public by issuing
treasury bonds. Most of these bonds are bought up by financial institutions
and corporations.

Are deficits good or bad? The answer is not simple. It depends on which
way you look at them. Thus in any gathering of economists you might hear
from some: Big budget deficits are bad because they push up interest rates
and will perpetuate a recession. From others you might hear: big budget

deficits are good because they add to purchasing power and will help end a recession.

The first reason why people think deficits are bad has to do with their unconscious sense that indebtedness is immoral. One can quote many statements, particularly from the last century, of religious leaders and presidents to the effect that a good person, and by implication a good government, did not live beyond its means. Modern society has different attitudes towards indebtedness. It operates on credit. Most upright Americans are at least indebted to their banks for the price of their home, for example. This experience of personal indebtedness ought to mitigate, somewhat, negative attitudes towards deficits.

In addition, it helps to keep in mind that deficits are quite a bit different than personal debts. Deficits really represent government investments. Businesses, when they spend in excess of their income, call that kind of spending investments. In 1980, the long-term debt of business in America was $912 billion.[11] Just as the individual homeowner has something to show for his/her mortgage, namely a house, just as businesses have something to show for their indebtedness, namely machines and buildings, so the federal government has something to show for its deficits, or investments. The government can point to its dams, roads, housing projects, museums, office buildings, and so forth. Beyond these it can point to a better educated and healthier, longer-living population.

Believe it or not, the government is in a better position than business in terms of its debt. The essential difference is this: government owes its money to people it has legal authority to tax, business owes its money to people from whom it has no way to recoup its finances. The money the government owes is taxable. In addition, it can meet its further financial obligations by further taxes.

Looked at as investments, government deficits are not so bad. This perspective also takes some of the onus off the complaint that we are indebting future generations. Theoretically, what we are also leaving them is a better world, according to our best knowledge.

But there is still a problem with deficits. If they are not all that bad, how large is too large? We really do not have an answer to that question. We know that countries with larger deficits than ours are continuing to grow economically,that is, their deficits have not hindered their growth.

But, we have generated a peculiar problem in the past few years. The Reagan administration, ideologically opposed to any deficits, has generated the largest deficits in the history of the nation. The following table indicates the growth of the federal deficits. It lists the highest deficits in the term of each of our recent presidents.[12]

There is a tendency among some economists to trivialize the importance of big budget deficits. Japan and West Germany, they point out correctly,

TABLE 1: Recent Budget Deficits

Fiscal Year	Administration	Deficit (billions)
1962	Kennedy	7.1
1966	Johnson	25.2
1972	Nixon	23.4
1976	Ford	66.4
1980	Carter	59.6
1982	Reagan	110.7
1983	Reagan	210.0

SOURCE: *Budget of the United States Government Fiscal Year 1985*

run big deficits as a percentage of their economies, and they have done all right. There are, however, some political and cultural differences between these countries and the U.S. which make direct borrowing of their social policies tricky for us, but they do indicate the possibility.[13]

It seems our recent large deficits have broken through the guidelines that economists use to predict their impact. Particularly worrisome is the long-term effect these deficits will have on the business community. The size of the impending deficits may frighten business away from investing. This would throw the country into another recession.

We need to bear in mind that decisions about deficits are decisions about national priorities. The deficit is not just what is left after we decide how much to put into other areas: food stamps, welfare, community development, etc. It operates like other budget decisions which affect how much of the national output goes into defense or the non-defense functions of the national government. Like the other budget decisions, it should be made by balancing our national interest in more private investment against our interest in more defense, or more help for the poor, or the re-building of cities, etc.

Conclusion

Taxes are the price we pay for public goods. As such they represent an investment we make in our social well-being and its national future. We can get a fair measure of the success of the allocation of these investments by looking at the outlay side of the federal budget.

If those concerned about the poor are disappointed, they are justly chagrined. We are not as generous as we might believe we are. The poor do not do very well on the outlay side of the budget.

But we can also have growth with equity. We cannot use budget deficits as an excuse for inadequate response to human need. It is possible to have economic growth with budget deficits. Those who do not believe this have merely to look around them. The evidence of economic growth is everywhere, and we have had budget deficits for years.

We ought, however, to be concerned about the size of these deficits, most particularly because there seems to be no general agreement about the impact of the huge, unprecedented deficits incurred by the Reagan Administration. How large is too large? We simply do not know. But, if we are going to incur deficits, it is time we gave the poor a chance to see what they can do with the equivalent of benefits we have so lavishly ravished on the rich.

Our efforts to help the poor are limited by the extent to which we can raise funds to meet the priorities we have for this purpose. Dealing with poverty is a tax issue among other things. Tax reform is not just a matter of raising more money. It also consists in evaluating our revenue raising

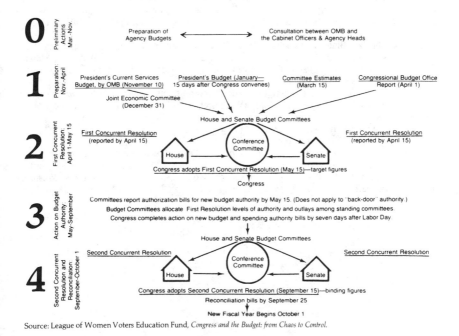

Source: League of Women Voters Education Fund, *Congress and the Budget: from Chaos to Control.*

methods to decide who benefits from the profits itself, and how the process
can be amended to meet the requirements of equity. Subsequent chapters
will take up these issues.

---

[1]Quoted in Paul F. Harstad, "Interpreting Americans' Attitudes toward Taxes," *Tax Notes*
(November 9, 1981), p. 1088.
[2]The rationale behind this realignment of the budgetary figures is given in chapter 4 of
Ronald D. Pasquariello, *Faith, Justice, and Our Nation's Budget: An Action Guide for
Christian Citizens* (Valley Forge, PA: Judson Press, 1982).
[3]A chart detailing the budget process appears at the end of this chapter.
[4]Budgetary figures in this chapter are from the *Budget of the United States Government,
Fiscal Year 1984,* and related documents.
[5]See Robert L. Heilbroner and Lester C. Thurow, *Economics Explained* (Englewood Cliffs,
N.J.: Prentice Hall, 1982), p. 66.
[6]Congressional Budget Office, *Balancing the Federal Budget and Limiting Federal
Spending: Constitutional and Statutory Approaches* (September, 1982), pp. 9-22. The gross
domestic product (GDP) is very similar to the GNP. The difference is that the GDP is based
on production within the borders of a country, while the GNP includes production and
income of all citizens of the country including those living abroad.
[7]Figures on poverty are taken from the Subcommittee on Oversight and Public Assistance
and Unemployment Compensation of the U.S. House Ways and Means Committee, *Background Material on Poverty* (Washington, D.C.: Government Printing Office, 1983), sections
2 and 4.
[8]Most of the data that follows is taken from Subcommittee on Oversight and Subcommittee
on Public Assistance and Unemployment Compensation of the U.S. House Ways and Means
Committee, *Families in Poverty: Changes in the 'Safety Net'*, (Washington, D.C.: Government Printing Office, 1984), *passim.*
[9]For a closer analysis of these figures, see Robert Greenstein, *The Significance of the
Administration's New Budget Proposals,* (Washington, D.C.: Center on Budget and Policy
Priorities, 1982).
[10]As reported in the *Washington Post,* January 1, 1983.
[11]See Heilbroner and Thurow, p. 95.
[12]Figures taken from *Budget of the United States Government, Fiscal Year 1983*
(Washington, D.C.: Government Printing Office, 1982), p. 9-62 and other current documents.
[13]For a careful analysis of the possibilities, see Robert Kuttner, *The Economic Illusion:
False Choices between Prosperity and Social Justice* (Boston: Houghton Mifflin, 1984), *passim.*

*If we want to redistribute income, the most
effective strategy is probably to redistribute
income.*

Christopher Jencks

Chapter 3:
Does the Tax System
Redistribute Wealth?

(On the Redistributive Effect of the Tax System)

Many Americans take for granted that the tax system redistributes
wealth, that economic monetary benefits go from the rich to the poor. This
perception is so ingrained in the our way of thinking about ourselves that
statements denying it are cavalierly brushed aside. Yet, a close look at the
figures indicate that taxes do not redistribute wealth, and that when the
whole system of government financing is taken into consideration—of
which taxation is a part—the system is such that the poor and the middle
class equivalently support the rich.

To support this claim, it is necessary to look first at taxation and wealth,
and then at federal fundraising programs as a whole.

Taxation and Wealth

i) The Distribution of Income

The idea of redistribution has taken hold in the society at large. A 1978
survey indicated that sixty percent of those polled favored income redistribution in one form or another, and only thirty-two percent opposed it
altogether.[1] Even those who would be most ideologically against the idea
accept it on pragmatic grounds: a modicum of redistribution contributes to
economic stability.

Yet there remains a tendency in the society at large to overestimate the
extent of redistribution because we underestimate the extent of the concentration of wealth. This perhaps has to do with the fact that the median

family income in America in 1982 was $19,446. This would mean that families with income above that figure are in the richest half of the country.

Or would it? The following table gives part of the answer.[2] It shows the distribution of income, the percentage of total money income, before taxes, received by each fifth of American families.

TABLE 1: Distribution of American Families' Income, 1982

Families, Ranked from Lowest to Highest Income	Income Range ($)	% Share of Total Income	
		1969	1982
Lowest fifth	0-10,000	4	4
Second fifth	10,000-17,000	11	9
Middle fifth	17,000-24,000	17	15
Fourth fifth	24,000-34,000	23	23
Highest fifth	34,000-	35	49

SOURCE: U.S. Census Bureau, 1981; *Federal Reserve Bulletin,* 1984

This table indicates that the distribution of family income has gotten a great deal more unequal since 1969. It shows that the top fifth of families had, in 1982, an income of about twelve times the bottom fifth. (In 1969, it was only nine times greater). Another way of looking at it: 20 percent of the families have close to half all income; the bottom group only about one-twenty-fifth of it.[3]

While the top fifth of all families has 49 percent of total income, most of them do not think of themselves as rich. Nor are they thought of as rich by the rest of society. In 1982, an income of about $34,000 placed a family in the top group. A husband and wife each earning a little more than $17,000 thus belong to the top fifth, but are they rich?

Okner and Pechman estimated the pre-tax distribution of income for the year 1966.[4] They report similar statistics. The top one-fifth of families got nearly half the total family income in the country. The bottom fifth got less than 4 percent. Furthermore, a still smaller group of Americans, the top 5 percent of families, recieved 33 percent of total income.

In addition, Okner and Pechman calculate that the income share of the top 1 percent, under their definition of income, was 11 percent. The average family among the top 1 percent of income earners receive nearly 60 times as much income as the average family in the bottom fifth.

ii) The Distribution of Wealth

This data on income, also suggests an extremely concentrated distribution of wealth. Private wealth is the value of an individual's property and possessions. It includes real estate, homes, cars, stocks trusts, retirement plans, etc. What are the facts about wealth? They are hard to come by. Wealth, unlike income, is not reported on tax returns. However, an investigation of the available statistics on wealth changes the picture quite considerably. The gap between the rich and the rest of us widens markedly.

A study by the University of Michigan Survey Research Center the 1970 distribution of wealth to be as follows:[5]

TABLE 2: 1970 Wealth Distribution of Families

Wealth Rank	% of Wealth
lowest fifth	less than 0.5
second fifth	1
middle fifth	5
fourth fifth	18
highest fifth	76

The study goes on further to say that the top five percent of families held forty percent of wealth, and the top one percent of wealth holders owned 25 percent of the wealth in 1970.

The most recent analysis of this kind of data, using slightly varying statistical aggregates of wealth, showed that this disparity continues and, if anything, is worsening. In an extensive 1983 study of Consumer Finances by the Federal Reserve System, the authors concluded that wealth is more heavily concentrated in a small number of families than family income. Their figures indicate that the top 2 percent of families hold 28 percent of net worth, and the top 10 percent hold 57 percent. The bottom 20 percent had a zero or negative net worth, indicating, in addition, that their hold on economic security is extremely fragile.[6]

The picture then changes significantly when one looks at wealth as opposed to income. The table verifies a major defect in our system of measuring economic well-being in this country. Since we most often measure income, not wealth, the rich appear to be less rich than they actually are. For example, while the top fifth of all families have almost 80 percent of total wealth, they have only 49 percent of total income.

In another series of studies, Smith and Franklin[7] came up with these figures for the "superrich."

TABLE 3: Share of Superrich in Wealth of All Persons, 1972

Asset	% Share Held By Superrich
Real estate	29.7
Corporate stock	66.7
State and local bonds	93.6
Corporate and foreign bonds	77.2
Savings bonds	39.6
Other federal bonds	97.6
Notes and mortgages	88.6
Cash	29.1
Business assets	37.7
Other assets	18.4
Number of persons	131.9 million

SOURCE: U.S. House Committee on the Budget, 1977

The superrich here are individual persons (not families) with gross assets of $60,000 or more in 1970 dollars. They were 5.6 percent of the adult population in 1969, and 6 percent in 1972. Hence they are a relatively stable portion of the population.

But this also means that 95 percent of the population did not have a net worth of $60,000 or more in 1972. Since these concentrations of wealth change relative little over the years, this is probably true today.

The concentration of wealth in the hands of the superrich is high for assets which lend to economic power and control. Take corporate stock. If the superrich own 66.7 percent of it, they potentially control the decision making related to all corporate assets. Add to this the fact that the rich marry the rich and the results are a great concentration of wealth in the hands of the few.

Taking this analysis one step further, Smith and Franklin show that in 1972 the top 1 percent of the wealthy individuals owned 25.9 percent of the wealth, while the top 0.5 percent of the wealthy owned 20.4 percent of the wealth. This wealth consisted of the following share of some important types of assets.[8]

TABLE 4: Share of Richest 0.5% and 1% of Persons in National Wealth, 1972

Asset	Shares Held by Richest	
	0.5%	1%
Real Estate	10.1	15.1
Corporate Stock	49.3	56.5
Bonds	52.2	60.0
Cash	8.5	13.5
Debt Instruments	39.1	52.7
Life Insurance	4.3	7.0
Trusts	80.0	89.9
Miscellaneous	6.8	9.8
Number of persons (millions)	1.04	2.09

SOURCE: U.S. House Committee on the Budget, 1977

Although statistics on the concentration of wealth in the hands of individuals are useful and informative, the wealth of households has greater relevance for assessing the distribution of economic power. It is estimated that there were 194,000 families in 1972 whose net worth was one million dollars or more. They accounted for only 0.3 percent of the nation's families, but held 14.6 percent of personal net wealth. As the following table shows, they held 60 percent of their wealth in corporate stock, which amounted to 35 percent of all personally held stock in the United States.[9] They also held 73 percent of state and local bonds (availing themselves of the preferential tax treatment of such bonds) and over two thirds of the marketable federal debt. These figures are rather sobering, particularly when one adverts to the fact that 55 percent of U.S. families had less than $10,000 and about 12 percent had less than $1000 in net worth during those years.

TABLE 5: Share of Millionaire Families in National Wealth, 1972

Asset	% Share	
Real Estate	5.3%	
Corporate Stock	35.2	
State and Local Bonds	72.9	
Corporate and Foreign Bonds	26.9	
Savings Bonds	8.6	
Other Federal Bonds	68.3	
Notes and Mortgages	24.0	
Cash	3.7	
Business Assets	11.3	
Other Assets	6.2	
Number of Families	194,073	.3%

SOURCE: U.S. House Committee on the Budget, 1977

These figures indicate the hazards of the concentration of wealth, particularly in a democracy. Wealth, as income, is highly concentrated. Wealth consolidation is more dangerous because control over economic resources represents political power. Where economic power is highly concentrated, it is safe to assume that political power, the power to shape the status quo and our corporate future, is also highly concentrated.

Despite feeble attempts at progressivity at the federal level, when all government taxes are considered—local, state and federal—there is little difference in before-tax and after-tax distribution of income. The following 1966 distributions are from estimates made by Pechman and Okner.[10]

TABLE 6: 1966 Percent Share of Income of Families

Income Rank	Before Tax	After Tax
Lowest fifth	3.88	4.34
Second fifth	10.04	10.31
Middle fifth	16.30	16.38
Fourth fifth	22.07	23.28
Highest fifth	47.71	45.69

SOURCE: Brookings Institution, *Who Bears the Burden,* 1974

Okner and Pechman demonstrated that the total tax system was proportional, that is, that after all taxes are paid (income, sales, property, payroll, etc.) individuals pay basically the same proportion of their income in taxes in most income groups. The system leaves the before-tax and after-tax income distribution relatively untouched. At best, the distribution has remained the same. Realistically, it has become more regressive. This appears to be the case because social security taxes, which are highly regressive, have continued to rise while the progressive elements of the tax system—personal tax, corporate tax and estate and gift taxes—have been reduced.

There is in addition to a concentration of wealth in our society also a concentration of tax savings. These are called tax expenditures and they will be discussed more fully in chapters eight and nine. These tax savings accrue mainly to high income individuals. They amounted to $365 billion in 1985.

The Anti-Progressivity of Government Fund Raising

Many Americans believe that taxation is the sole means by which government raises money to support its activities. And, for most of our history, that supposition was essentially correct. However, within the last two decades particularly, the government has increasingly turned to nontax sources to raise a considerable amount of funds. They include: "federal and federally assisted borrowing" and "tax expenditures." These activities are "anti-progressive." They are anti-progressive because the government has to pay for the funds it raises, it has to pay for them to high income individuals, and it has to pay for them from the taxes it raises from the rest of the taxpaying population.

The following table might help to clarify this discussion.[11]

TABLE 7: Government Fund Raising, 1985

Source	Receipts (in billions)
1. Individual Income Tax	$328.4
2. Corporate Tax	76.5
3. Excise Tax	38.4
4. Estate and Gift Taxes	5.6
5. Customs Duties	9.4
6. Miscellaneous Receipts	16.0
7. Social Insurance Taxes	270.7
8. Federal & Federally Assisted Borrowing	274.3
9. Tax Expenditures	365.1

SOURCE: Joint Committee on Taxation, 1984; *Budget of the United States Government Fiscal Year 1985*

Items 1-7 in the preceding table fall under the category of taxes: "Social Insurance Taxes" consists mostly of the payroll tax. "Miscellaneous Receipts" include such items as interest, rents, royalties and the sale of government property, products and services. The items of concern to this discussion are 8 and 9. They total almost one-half of federal fund-raising.

i) Federal and Federally Assisted Borrowing

Federal and federally assisted borrowing includes borrowing from the public to cover the federal deficit, and the credit the government advances in direct loans, guaranteed loans, government sponsored enterprise loans, and other credit programs.

The federal government provides credit to individuals, businesses, institutions, localities and foreign governments. The major mechanisms it uses for this activity are either direct loans or loan guarantees.[12] There is an element of subsidy involved in any of these federal credit programs since assistance is given in terms more favorable than in private institutions. Suppose the interest rate banks are charging is 13 percent, and the government offers a more favorable 11.5 percent to those who can qualify for it. The difference is 1.5 percent. On a loan of $100,000, simple interest at 1.5 percent would come to $1500. That would be the interest subsidy the borrower would be receiving from the government.

Since the interest rates the government charges are usually lower than the going market rate, the difference between the market rate and the government supported interest rate amounts to an interest subsidy to the borrower. These interest subsidies are equivalent to cash grants to the borrower.[13] Figures on the total amount of these interest rate subsidies are not available. It can be safely assumed that the subsidies go to high income individuals because it is they who make the loans.

Another revenue raising activity of the federal government with similar effect is borrowing from the public to pay off the national debt. In this case, the federal government borrows cash to meet current outlays not covered by receipts from taxation (i.e., to cover the annual deficit), and to refinance the maturing debt.

Public debt is held by financial institutions, private individuals, corporations, state and local governments, foreign and international investors. All these are essentially high income individuals.

In 1982 the government borrowed $135.0 billion from the public. Almost all of this amount, $127.9 billion, was used to finance the government deficit. The remaining $7.1 billion went to finance the other means of revenue raising.

Gross federal debt has risen substantially over the past decades, from $270.8 billion in 1954 to $1,147.0 billion in 1982. It has increased at an average annual rate of about 6 percent.

Interest on the debt held by the public has risen much faster than the debt itself, due to the strong upward trend in interest rates. Consequently, whereas the federal debt held by the public increased by four times between 1954 and 1982, the interest paid on this debt increased nineteen times.

ii) Tax Expenditures

Tax expenditures are defined in the Budget Act of 1974 as the revenue losses attributable to provisions of the tax law that allow "a special exclusion, exemption or deduction from gross income or which provide a special credit, a preferential rate of tax, or a deferral of tax liability." Generally known as tax loopholes, they are special exemptions written into law which apply to a limited class of persons only. In 1983, there were 104 separate tax expenditures.

Tax expenditures are similar in effect to direct spending programs. Because they represent funds the government is, by law, entitled to, but, again by law, decided not to collect, they add to the federal deficit in the same way that direct spending programs do. And since tax expenditures allocate funds for certain types of activity (home mortgage deductions, accelerated depreciation for business projects, etc.), they are not simply revenue lost. They are equivalently funds raised by the government for particular projects. The government could just as well have collected these funds and returned them to the taxpayers to spend for specific purposes.[14] Tax expenditures too are anti-progressive, because they accrue to high income individuals. This issue will be discussed further in chapters eight and nine.

Conclusion

This chapter examined the redistributive effect of the federal tax system, and found it wanting. The federal tax system is at best proportional, though the worst case scenario is probably true, namely, that it is regressive due to the increasing growth of social security taxes, the continued reduction of progressive elements like the corporation tax, and the expansion of anti-progressive elements. This alone needs to be a cause for concern for persons interested in equity, equality, and the suffering and empowerment of the poor, because the tax system is the chief means by which we redistribute wealth in this country. It is our major corporate mechanism for distributive justice. The outlay side of the budget, which contains our "social spending" programs, is dependent on the tax system for the revenue for these programs. Ultimately, because the tax system is not redistributive, it is the poor and middle-income class who are paying for the funding of these programs.

This becomes clear when we take a long look at the other means of government fund-raising, of which the tax system is a part.

We spoke also in this chapter about three government revenue raising activities. One was the raising of funds for its loan making programs. In this case we pointed out that the loans go mainly to high income individuals, and are equivalently a subsidy amounting to the difference in the amount of interest on the loan that the government obligates itself to cover. A second was the interest on the public debt, which the government must pay on the funds it borrows to cover its deficit operations. This interest too is owed to high income individuals. The third is the category of tax expenditures, which benefit the 30 percent of Americans who itemize their tax returns. These are again high income individuals.

Our argument is that since these revenue raising activities, the results of which accrue to high income individuals, must be paid out of the tax system, they are anti-progressive. They are anti-progressive because they equivalently reduce the tax burden of high income individuals, and because the taxes of the lower and middle-income class must be raised to meet these obligations. The consequence of all this is that government fund raising requires the poor and middle class to make indirect payments, through the mechanism of the tax system, to the rich.

Beyond the issue of the redistribution of wealth, there is also the weighty question of the distribution of power. The syllogism is simple: concentrations of wealth mean concentrations of economic power, and concentrations of economic power mean concentrations of political power. Federal credit programs play a significant role in allocating our economic resources. Important questions remain unanswered about the impact and distribution of benefits and costs of credit assistance. It is not clear what effect this allocation has on important economic issues such as employment, production, and economic growth.

Wealth concentrations need to be reduced not just because they allow consumption inequalities, but because they foster inordinate economic and political control. Christians concerned about the condition of the poor need to give this issue serious consideration. The maldistribution of wealth is a cause of poverty they, and the rest of the country, have not yet faced. This aspect of poverty can only be dealt with through the tax system.

[1]Reported in Harstad, p. 1094.

[2]It is based on data taken from U.S. Bureau of the Census, *Current Population Reports,* Series p-60, #127, (August, 1981), p. 15; and Robert B. Avery, Gregory E. Elliehausen and Glenn B. Canner, "Survey of Consumer Finances, 1983," *Federal Reserve Bulletin* (September, 1984), p. 681, table 2.

[3]*Tax Notes* (July 30, 1984), p. 506 reported that the top one-fifth of all households received 41.8% of all income after taxes in 1982. It also noted that the after-tax income of the poorest fifth declined between 1980 and 1982.

⁴Benjamin Okner and Joseph A. Pechman, *Who Bears the Tax Burden?* (Washington, D.C.: Brookings Institution, 1974), p. 46.

⁵Gene E. Mumy, "Financing Federal Budget Expenditures," in Marcus G. Raskin (ed.), *The Federal Budget and Social Reconstruction,* (Washington, D.C.: Institute for Policy Studies, 1978), p. 74.

⁶Robert B. Avery, Gregory E. Elliehausen and Glenn B. Cannon, "Survey of Consumer Finances, 1983: A Second Report," *Federal Reserve Bulletin* (December, 1984), p. 863.

⁷James Smith and Stephen Franklin, "Prepared Statement" in *Data on Distribution of Wealth in America.* Hearings before the House Task Force on Distributive Impacts of Budget and Economic Policies of the Committee on the Budget (Washington, D.C.: Government Printing Office, 1977), p. 177.

⁸Smith and Franklin, p. 174.

⁹Smith and Franklin, p. 181.

¹⁰Okner and Pechman, p. 56.

¹¹Items 1-8 are from *The Budget of the United States Government, Fiscal Year 1985;* Item 9 is from the Joint Committee on Taxation, *Estimate of Federal Tax Expenditures, 1984-1989* (Washington, D.C.: Government Printing Office, 1984).

¹²See James M. Bickley, "Federal Credit Control and the Distribution of Federal Credit by Policy Objectives," in *Studies in Taxation, Public Finance and Related Subjects—A Compendium, Volume 6* (Washington, D.C.: Fund for Public Policy Research, 1982), pp. 181-193, for a thorough discussion of these issues.

¹³This is generally accepted as fact. See, for example, *Special Analysis, The Budget of the U.S. Government, Fiscal Year 1981,* p. 141.

¹⁴See Mumy, p. 46.

Anatole France

Chapter 4:
Some Taxing Criteria
(On Criteria for Judging the Fairness of the Tax System)

What is a fair tax? Some say that this is a question that is impossible to answer. They will point to all the possible problems in deciding what a fair tax is: whether taxes should be on income or wealth, on consumption or income, on all persons without distinction or differentially according to one's ability-to-pay, on short term or long term investment incentives and so forth.

We cannot of course give in to that kind of discouragement. There are some things one can say about a fair tax. One can define the elements that must be present for a tax to be fair, even though one is constrained to admit that there is no ultimate definition. More about this in a moment.

At this point we need to make an important clarification: whether our taxes are fair or not is an ethical, not an economic question. The answer to the question that possesses us at the moment depends on our social objectives. It is because the public holds conflicting opinions about those objectives, that the answer is difficult to discern. It is the role of ethics to tell us what kind of society we should have, and it is up to economics to tell us how we can most easily achieve that goal. Ethical questions about the good and the just will ultimately determine what a fair tax is. The answer to our question will be qualified by our moral assumptions.

We dealt with some of these assumptions in the first chapter of this book. The principles, or values, of participation, justice and mutual love can all be subsumed under the concept of shalom.

Shalom, Gerhard von Rad tells us, means communal well-being, and almost always has a material emphasis to it.[1] Jeremiah brings out the subtle-

41

ties of the concept in this verse: "Seek the shalom of the city to which I
have sent you, and pray to the Lord for it, because on its shalom depends
your shalom." (Jer. 27,9). Here the prophet links the well-being of the
Jewish exiles to the well-being of the city, Babylon, to which they have
been exiled. Individual and communal well-being are a joint act—one does
not happen without the other. The way to shalom lies in collaboration, in
joining with others in social acts to establish the promised communal well-
being.

The Bible, in its realism, recognizes that this is the future society, the
society by which the present is to be shaped. In its realism it also recognizes
that the present society must be shaped by its concern for the poor. Without the option for the poor, there is no communal well-being, no shalom.

The tax system is one among a number of levers of transformation of
this present society, so it is one of the social mechanisms that falls within
the scope of our biblical concerns. What specific criteria are we to bring to
it?

A fair tax, from our perspective, would tax all income, and tax according
to ability-to-pay. Where possible, it would redistribute income from the rich
to the poor. It would also be simple and efficient. Many of these criteria are
accepted by economists generally, though interpretations of their meaning
vary, often depending on the particular perspective of the economist in
question.

Taxing All Income

We raised this issue in the chapter on the redistribution of wealth. We
pointed out there that the present system hardly touches wealth, and mana-
ges to exclude a great deal of income from the tax collector's reach.

There are various definitions of income. For example, every taxpayer
knows that the system as we now have it taxes a reduced mass of income,
referred to as "adjusted gross income" and "taxable income." Adjusted
gross income is generally defined as gross income minus business
deductions. Taxable income results from a further set of itemized deductions and exemptions.

Musgrave offers this definition of income, which is also employed by
many tax reformers. Income includes "all additions to a person's wealth
over a given period no matter from what source (wages or capital), in whatever form (cash, accrued or non-market), or how used (consumed or
saved)."[2] He goes on to point out that the present level of taxable income
falls 40 percent short of this. Exclusions and deductions account for this

shortfall. This definition excludes the taxation of currently held wealth, but is all-encompassing enough to include all income.

There are some assumptions in this criterion which should be stated at the outset. It makes the judgment that income—rather than consumption, for example—is the best measure of taxpaying capacity. This more or less ranks as a tradition in the U.S. context. It hinges on the ability-to-pay principle, which is the basis of the idea of progressivity in taxation. It simply states that persons with a high ability-to-pay have a higher stake in the system than those who do not. Utilizing the system more, they should be required to make a higher contribution toward the government spending involved in enhancing and maintaining the system.

History is on the side of this position. Adam Smith, the father of free market capitalism, argued in 1776 that "the subjects of every state ought to contribute towards the support of the government as nearly as possible in proportion to their respective abilities." He also said: "The expense of government to the individuals of a great nation, is like the expense of management to the joint tenants of a great estate, who are obliged to contribute in proportion to their respective interests in the estate."[3] The more one has, the bigger one's stake in the social order, and therefore the more expense of maintaining and protecting that order the taxpayer should bear.

A second assumption in this criterion is that the advantages of equity this broad definition of income would bring to the tax system outweigh the benefits accruing to individuals because of exclusions, deductions and credits. Our rationale for this, which will be discussed more fully in chapter nine, is that needed exceptions should be made on the outlay side, not the tax side, of the federal budget.

Redistributing Income

Just the idea of redistribution raises the hackles of some folks. They view a person's income as essentially the fruit of her/his own labor and resources. They believe that the government should have very little role in equalizing the amounts which individuals acquire, since individuals are entitled to whatever income arises from their own labor or property. Our view (as explained in chapter one) is that labor and property have value because of the framework established by society. And the society has therefore a right to tax the income earned for the continuous improvement of the social framework. The question of what that improvement consists of is an ethical one, and its answer is subject to some debate. However, as indicated in the last chapter, most Americans agree that the tax system should redistribute income.

The reader needs to bear in mind that there is a limit to the amount of distribution that can happen through the taxing of income. It is an open question whether income redistribution can meet the standards set by the Bible in its option for the poor. To achieve the kind of redistribution that we believe is required by the Bible, the system would have to tax not only income, but also wealth. The taxation of wealth, however, is sufficiently controversial to postpone its consideration to another book. A necessary first step in the kind of justice that interests us, however, would be this proposal: that the tax system be so comprehensive that it reaches all income.

Taxing According to Ability-to-Pay

To most people—those who favor a progressive tax system, tax justice means taxing according to ability-to-pay, and that means that taxes should be progressive. There are three terms which usually are dragged into the ring when economists raise the issue of fairness. They are progressivity, regressivity, proportionality. To this we add a fourth term, anti-progressivity, which refers to some of the new directions fiscal policy has taken in the last two decades.

i) Progressivity

A tax is progressive if its rate is larger on those who have a lot of the thing taxed than it is on those who have little.

Progressivity is usually defined in terms of income. A progressive income tax is one that simply would take a higher percentage of income from the rich than from the poor. The federal income tax illustrates a progressive rate structure. The rates on unmarried individuals in 1983 rose from 12 percent on the first $3,400 of taxable income to 14 percent on the next $1,000, to 16 percent on the next $2,100 and so on up to 50 percent on all income over $55,300.

Property taxes can be progressive if the rate varies with the amount of property owned. A progressive property tax would be higher for someone with $100,000 worth of property and less for someone with $24,000 worth. A sales tax could be progressive if the tax rate increased with the size of the sale. A purchase for $1,000 would be taxed at 10 percent, a sale of $25 at 1 percent. The sales tax could also be made progressive by regulating what it taxes. Thus it would be progressive if it did not apply to foods and medicines, but did apply to attorney's fees and real estate brokers' fees, which tend to be used more often by high income persons.

Permit fees could be made progressive by charging rates proportional to the size of the business, rather than charging the same rate to all businesses. They could also be made progressive by excluding certain types of businesses.

ii) Regressivity

As you might expect, a regressive tax is just the opposite of a progressive tax. A tax is regressive if its rate is larger on those who have little of the thing taxed than it is on those who have a lot. The social security tax is a perfect example of a regressive tax. Workers in 1985 making $39,600 a year paid $2,972 which is 7.05 percent of their income. Meanwhile an executive pulling in $100,000 a year paid the same $2,972 which is about three percent of his/her income.

General sales taxes are very regressive, because low and middle income Americans must use a higher percent of their income for the goods and services taxed. While only 40 percent of the income of the well-to-do goes to the purchase of basic necessities (food, clothing, housing, medical care), 80-90 percent of the income of the poor goes to those purchases. Sales taxes are usually on these items.

Excise taxes are even more regressive. Most are single rate or flat taxes: 24 cents on a pack of cigarettes, or 30 cents on a gallon of gas. Rich and poor pay the same amount of tax, though that sum is a much smaller percent of the income of the rich.

For the obvious reason that regressive taxes impinge more on the poor, and low and middle-income Americans than they do on the rich, regressivity does not mesh with the principles articulated in this book.

iii) Proportionality

Proportional taxes are taxes in which everyone, rich and poor, is taxed at the same rate. Another way of putting it: They take equal proportions of income from all taxpayers.

Most recently the proportional tax on income has appeared under the guise of the flat rate tax. In one form this would impose the same rate, 20 percent on all incomes. It means the person who earns $10,000 would pay $2,000 in taxes, and the person who earns $100,000 would pay $20,000 in income taxes.

On the surface, proportional taxes seem right. They spread the misery around equally, according to one federal official. So what could be more fair? That is deceptive argumentation.

In the first place, that $2,000 is more important to the person earning $10,000 than is the $20,000 to the person earning $100,000. This is because the person earning $10,000 spends a greater percentage of his/her salary on basic necessities. Each dollar has a greater impact on the livelihood, quality of life and well-being of lower income persons than higher income persons.

In the second place, the flat rate tax assumes that the pre-tax distribution of wealth is just. We pointed out in the last chapter that it is not. The flat tax does not mesh with our principles, because taking the same percentage from income leaves individuals in the same relative position regarding income. It simply does not redistribute income.

iv) Anti-progressivity

This is not a term that you will find in many text books, but it is one that has been called forth by recent government activities in need of a name. It was used and explained in the preceding chapter.

The net effect of the new government efforts at fund raising has been to indebt it to high income persons. This is because the interest the government must pay for the money it borrows goes to high income individuals. That interest is paid for out of taxes drawn from the rest of the population. This amounts to taking from the lower class to give to the rich. This activity is anti-progressive, not just regressive. By paying this interest to high income individuals on the money it borrows, it effectively reduces the tax they pay.

There is another anti-progressive tendency in current government financial operations. It is the tendency to replace progressive taxes with regressive ones. One example is the legislation reducing estate and gift taxes—which are progressive because they impact principally the well-to-do—and raising excise and payroll taxes, which are regressive taxes. Because they reduce the progressivity of the system, these changes are anti-progressive.

Other anti-progressive moves have to do with weak enforcement of the tax code (because most of the tax evaders are among those with high income), and shifting tax burdens to the states and municipalities (because their revenue raising procedures are regressive.)

Efficiency

Taxes are an intrusion. Simply because they take some of our financial resources, they intrude upon our lives and alter them in some way. A goal of tax policy—and a desire of most taxpayers—is that they should intrude as little as possible. An efficient tax is one that reduces the amount of distortion or intrusion while achieving its effect or purpose.

There are a number of debates about which taxes are efficient and which are not. Again, it all depends on the kind of society the debater wants. Take the cigarette law. Cigarettes are dangerous to the health of the smoker, and of the non-smoker in the same room. Cigarettes are also highly taxed. The tax can have two effects on the smoker. Giving up cigarettes will reduce the overall tax she/he pays. In addition, it could cause some to smoke less than they would if cigarettes were cheaper.

Because of its positive effects, some would consider this tax efficient. Tobacco growers and farm workers would probably not agree. For them the tax is inefficient because it reduces tobacco consumption, thereby distorting the working of the free market for a questionable social purpose.

Another example: Because the costs of homeownership are tax deductible, more persons buy and own their own home. Homeowners and the housing industry would consider this efficient. Renters would not. Nor would center city dwellers, mayors, and a host of other urbanites who are suffering because of urban sprawl from a shrinking tax base.

Efficiency is a difficult criterion to apply. Is the tax code more efficient when it encourages oilwell drilling, charitable contributions, home buying, etc.? People can disagree about the intention, but all can agree on this: a tax is efficient if it achieves the purpose for which it was designed with as little dislocation as possible of our resources.

Efficiency often comes in conflict with equity, and always requires a judgment call. A tax may be efficient, i.e. achieve its goal with a minimum of economic distortion, but it may do so by favoring one group of taxpayers over others. The "Capital Formation theorists" (discussed in chapter 9) argue that equity has to give way to efficiency. However, we will argue later that we can have equity and economic growth. A major goal of the tax system, nevertheless, should be to reduce inefficiency as low as possible.

Simplicity

The simplicity of a tax is gauged by how well taxpayers understand it and how easily they can comply with its provisions. Surprisingly, simplifying tax forms is not a public priority. In a 1979 H&R Block study, changing tax laws was favored over simplifying forms by nearly a five-to-one ratio. Only 11 percent of those polled were interested in simplifying forms.[4] But simplicity needs to be a serious concern. It is not only a question of simplifying tax forms, but of simplifying the system itself. If it is too complex for individuals to understand, then it is unfair. A law needs to be understood if it is to be enforceable. So also the tax system. It is so complex that the current director of the IRS admitted that his agency could not train personnel to deal adequately with a few of the most complex returns. Its present complexity makes the system accessible only to those who can afford to hire tax lawyers to work through the tax maze.

Another problem with the complexity of the present system is that it demands a large amount of resources to administer. This requires that the IRS have a large staff to insure that taxpayers calculate tax liability correctly. The bill payer in this case is the taxpayer. In addition, the complexity of the system, and the many possibilities for tax avoidance, have diverted the energies of thousands into the business of filling out tax forms or constructing schemes for tax shelters. A millionaire who has to pay taxes, it is said, ought to fire his/her tax lawyer. Adding insult to injury, the tax code has made the services of these high-priced lawyers tax deductible. It is the public, then, which pays for at least half the services of these experts in tax avoidance.

Compexity also undermines the perception of the individual taxpayer that the system is equitable. The ability of the well-to-do to avoid taxes is widely publicized. Taxpayers realize that these individuals are paying less taxes, not because they have a lower ability-to-pay, but because they have better access to knowledge about the details of the system. These feelings contribute to the sense that the system is unfair.

In terms of compliance, the simplest tax would be to charge everyone the same dollar amount for the privilege of being American. This tax, however, would also be very unfair, as we indicated above, because it would impinge heavily on lower-income taxpayers. It is generally agreed that we can get more fairness by sacrificing some simplicity to equity and efficiency. Americans can deal with a bit more complexity than a simple one rate or flat rate system. They have shown themselves skillful at manipulating many parts of the present system in the last hours of April 15.

Conclusion

In this chapter, we have laid out these five criteria for evaluating the tax system and individual taxes:

1. The system should tax all income.

2. The system should redistribute income.

3. The system should be progressive.

4. Taxes should be efficient.

5. The system should be simple.

Each one of these criteria has been carefully nuanced to mesh with the principles of justice and shalom. That all income be taxed, means that no exclusions be allowed. Special needs ought to be compensated for on the outlay side of the budget, where they can be carefully monitored to meet our national priorities. That the system should redistribute income means that the after-tax distribution of income be more just (i.e., wealth be less concentrated to the degree that the society meets the criteria of justice, sustainability and participation) than the before-tax distribution of income.

That the system be progressive means that high income persons pay a greater share of their income in taxes than lower income persons, and that anti-progressive elements in government financing be eliminated. efficiency and simplicity call for taxes that achieve their purpose and a system that is understandable and easily complied with.

---

[1] See "Eirene" in *Theological Wordbook of the New Testament, vol. 2,* edited by G. Kittel and G. Freidrich (Grand Rapids, MI: Eerdmans, 1964), p. 406 and *passim.*

[2] Richard A. Musgrave, "Tax Reform—1981 and After," in *Economic Choices: Studies in Tax/Fiscal Policy,* Francis M. Bator, Richard Musgrave (Washington, D.C.: Center for National Policy, 1982), p. 15.

[3] Quoted in Brandon, Rowe, and Stanton, p. 4.

[4] Harstad, p. 1093.

*The political problem of mankind is to
combine three things: Economic Efficiency, Social Justice and Individual Liberty*
John Maynard Keynes

Chapter 5:
Who Bears the Burden
of the Tax System?

(An Analysis Showing that the Middle Class
Bears the Burden)

Is the tax burden equitably distributed? Does each American bear
his/her fair share? The answer to these questions is no. It is the middle
class who bears the burden of the tax system. Those who have not thought
about the tax system carefully may be surprised by this assertion, though
the preceding pages of this book should have suggested it to them. This
chapter gathers together evidence to support this claim. Some of what is
going to be said will be repeated in different forms in later chapters. The
repitition is necessary to help the reader understand where the weight of
the tax system falls, and the resulting unfairness of the system.

The Anger of the American People

The American People are angry. A great deal of that anger is directed at
the American tax system. Why?

Some of that anger has to do with history—the fact that this nation's
birth trauma was a tax revolt. It is part of our culture and tradition to
dislike taxes.

But it is also true that most Americans alive today are descended from
immigrant families that stepped onto our shores more than a century after
the American Revolution. Many of these immigrants, however, were of a
special type. They tended to be the rugged individuals who, dissatisfied
with conditions in their homelands, were willing to withstand the rigors of
uprootedness for the sake of the satisfactions they sought.

So history is part of the problem. But is there something more? There would seem to be. Consider this: Tax burdens are higher in many other nations. Among twenty-three Western industrial nations, the U.S. ranks seventh lowest in the amount of revenues it collects (as a percentage of Gross Domestic Product). Only Australia, Greece, Portugal, Japan, Spain and Turkey raise less taxes.[1]

Among these nations, tax compliance varies. Sweden, with the highest pool of tax revenues, has the highest compliance; Italy, near the bottom of the scale, has a low rate of compliance.

Another way to get a perspective on whether or not taxes are too high, is to look at the amount of "disposable personal income" Americans have after taxes. In the 1940's, real disposable personal income averaged $4,709 per person (calculated in what the dollar was worth in 1982). The average for the first three years of the 1980's was $9,363. This is almost exactly double. In other words, while government was taking more money, the portion of national income people had to spend or save was doubling.[2]

From another perspective, it bears emphasizing that taxes are not too high if they buy what Americans want as a nation. Social security taxes, for example, enjoy a special tolerance among American taxpayers. A poll compared them to other taxes. The respondents were asked how much they object to these taxes " . . . considering what we receive . . . "[3]

Social security was the preferred tax, with 66 percent having little or no objection and only 28 percent, little more than one quarter of the respondents, having serious objections. The gasoline tax was unpopular because gas prices were soaring at the time (the poll was taken in 1978). Sales taxes were less unpopular.

Harstad speculates that the reason for the popularity of social security was that "taxpayers perceive a direct link between social security taxes and benefits—indeed the higher their taxes the greater their eventual benefits."[4] The data seem to indicate that it is not the amount of taxes, but the return on their taxes that is important to Americans. This would suggest that Americans believe that a fair tax is one in which they perceive they get a fair return for their tax investment.

Tax evasion has become as American as Mom, apple pie, and the home computer. The IRS has figured that out of the estimated $750 billion that U.S. taxpayers were supposed to pay, about $100 billion would not be payed in 1983.[5] The change has been dramatic. This is up from only $29 billion in 1973 (amounting to an increase of 53 percent adjusting for inflation). The future offers more of the same.

For some reason, waitresses seem to get the blame for all this tax avoidance. Time and time again, they are cited as examples of tax avoidance for not reporting their tips. The facts seem to indicate otherwise. It is not the working class, but the white middle class and upper class who are the tax evaders. The breakdown according to IRS is as follows: Unreported income from individual business activities amounts to $26 billion; from crime, it is $6-10 billion; from capital gains, $9.1 billion; from dividends and interest, $7.7 billion; and from profits from partnerships and small business, $7.2 billion.[6]

"Crime" includes such activities as drug traficking, gambling, numbers, prostitution, pornography. IRS might want to consider other means of rectifying this discrepancy than trying to collect taxes for these activities. Unreported income from individual business activities is the big item. The under-reporters in this category include doctors, contractors who work off the books and farmers. These are the stars in the tax evasion sweepstakes.

The question is, why do they do it? There seems to be no definitive answers, though studies suggest a reasonable conclusion. The CPA institute, which devoted two years to a study of the question, offer the following list:

1. A sense that one's tax burden has risen above its fair share.

2. Erosion of public confidence that the tax law is treating everyone fairly, due primarily to the increasing complexity of tax regulations.

3. A sense that tax loopholes are unfair.[7]

Two other elements which are often factored in: greed and the everybody-does-it syndrome. These two may be part of the picture, but they are minor. Greed has always been part of human nature, even when tax conformity was high. "Everybody-does-it" indeed motivates some human behavior, but not extensively. It does not penetrate deeply into the area of sexual mores, for example, though we may superficially think so.

Ultimately, the anger of the American taxpayer towards the tax system seems to come from the perceived unfairness of the system. That is the common denominator in all three of the elements listed above. Is this anger justified?

Tax Imbalances

Americans look at the income tax. They see the rates getting large as the scale of income levels rise, and they assume that taxes are progressive. The reality of U.S. tax policy is quite different from this appearance. The net effect of U.S. taxes is not progressive.

i) The Personal Income Tax

There is a difference between the rate structure created by law (nominal rate) and the actual rate (effective rate) people end up paying. The nominal or statutory rate is the book rate, the rate we think others pay on their gross income. But as anyone who has filled out a tax form knows, there are exceptions, exemptions, deductions and the like. The "effective rate" is what a person or persons actually pay, after all exemptions, loopholes, deductions are accounted for. The graph below illustrates how special exclusions reduce tax progressivity.[8]

The nominal or statutory rates are represented by the steeply sloped solid line at the top of the figure. They appear progressive, though they rise much more rapidly for lower incomes than higher. The effective rates—what people actually pay—are represented by the bottom broken-

FIGURE 1: Influence of Various Provisions on Effective Rates of the Federal Individual Income Tax, 1976: All Taxpayers

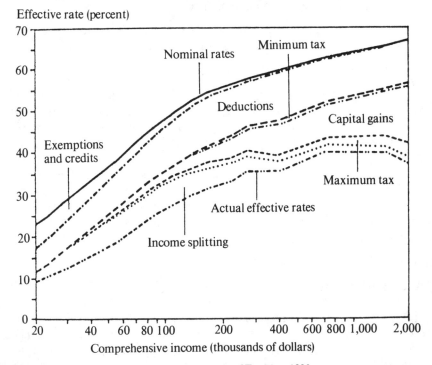

SOURCE: Brookings Institution, *The Economics of Taxation*, 1980.

dotted line. Compare these two lines. The nominal rates move from about 23 percent on the lowest incomes to more than 65 percent on the highest. The effective rates are not as steep. They rise more gradually from about 10 percent to less than 40 percent and then actually decline slightly. They are no longer progressive. Persons with the highest incomes pay less than those preceding them on the income scale. The intermediary lines on the graph indicate how much particular provisions cause the rates to drop at each income level.

All told, taxes on the rich are not as high as they appear to be at first glance. In 1980, for example, income taxes as a proportion of total money income was about 2 percent for incomes around $7,500, 10 percent around $10,000, and 20 percent around incomes of $40,000. They reached a high of 33 percent for incomes of $200,000. But they actually declined to 32 percent for incomes over $500,000.[9] The data for 1982 indicate the further skewing of the tax. While the number of households with incomes of $50,000 or more increased by 24 percent, that income bracket paid only 5 percent more in federal income taxes.[10]

ii) Payroll Taxes

Payroll, or social security taxes, are very regressive. The richer a person gets, the lower the percentage of one's income one has to pay in payroll taxes. This is because the taxes are levied as a flat percentage on all wages up to a ceiling. Above the ceiling, wages are entirely free of tax.

For example, in 1984, the flat percentage was 6.7 percent and the wage ceiling was $37,800. Anyone making that salary would pay 6.7 percent of it in taxes. A corporation executive, on the other hand, making $500,000 would pay the same amount—6.7 percent on his first $37,800 in wages— but that would come to only 0.5 percent of his/her very generous salary. Because of this ceiling, the rate for those making more than $37,800 is lower than those making less than that. This means that the effective rates—the rate people actually pay—is higher for lower and middle-income Americans than for the rich! Remember, payroll taxes are on wages only. All forms of capital are exempt from it.

Social security has always been a regressive tax. And over the years, it has grown larger, while the more progressive taxes have either declined or not grown as rapidly. The following table gives the picture. Social security taxes have grown (as a percentage of the GNP), while all other taxes in the aggregate have declined, and continue to do so. The bulk of non-social security taxes are progressive. It is the evident rise in social security taxes that "is the sole reason for the increase in the overall tax burden."[11]

TABLE 1: Social Security Taxes and Non-Social Security Taxes as a Percent of GNP, Selected Years

Year	Social Security Taxes	Non-Social Security Taxes
1955	1.3	16.0
1960	2.1	16.5
1965	2.5	15.2
1970	3.9	16.0
1975	5.0	13.9
1980	5.3	14.8
1982	5.9	14.5

SOURCE: *Budget of the United States Government,* Selected Years

These regressive taxes are becoming a larger and larger burden on low-income earners. By 1977, the social security payroll tax became the highest tax paid by about two-thirds of the nation's income recipients. This means, of course, that it became a disproportionately larger share of the income of those who earned less than the established ceiling.

Another instructive example of the growing regressivity of the federal tax system is the view from the median American income. The median income is the middle income, half of the Americans make more than it, half make less than it. If it goes up or comes down, there are still half Americans above it and half below it. When the two basic federal taxes paid by individuals—the income tax and the payroll tax—are combined and compared over time, the results are as shown in Table 2.[12]

The chart indicates that in 1955, according to the Treasury Department, a four-person family with one earner making half the median income (that would be the lowest 25 percent) faced an average tax rate of 4 percent. For a similar family making twice the median income (the top income quarter) the tax was 12.4 percent. The rate of the more affluent family was just over three times that of the poorer family.

Things changed by 1982. The family in the bottom quarter had an average tax rate of 20.1 percent. The family in the top quarter had a tax rate of 25.9 percent. In 27 years the three to one ratio had fallen to not quite a 1.3 to one ratio! And families in the top half were paying almost the

same rate. In addition, the family in the bottom quarter experienced a five-
fold increase in their tax burden; the family in the top quarter saw it just
about double.

These facts point to the continuing regressivity of the federal tax system.
But there is more.

TABLE 2: How Progressive Is Our Tax System?

Income	Tax Rate (Percent)	
Twice Medium	12.4	25.9
Medium	8.9	24.6
Half Medium	4.0	20.1
Year	1955	1982

SOURCE: *The Washington Post,* 1983

iii) The Corporation Tax

The tax on corporations' net profits in the years before World War II
often produced more revenue than the individual income tax or any other
tax. It quickly fell to second place, behind the individual income tax, after
the war. In the late 1960's it was overtaken by the payroll taxes. By 1980 it
yielded only 12.4 percent of federal revenue: less than half that came
from payroll taxes. This decline continues. The 1981 Tax Act virtually
eliminated the tax for many corporations.

While it is generally admitted that the tax is progressive, it is very difficult to tell which income class actually bears how much of the burden of
this tax. However, the continuing decline of the tax is having the effect of
contributing to the overall regressivity of the system.

iv) Other Federal Taxes

Other federal taxes are small. Estate and gift taxes are considered
progressive because they fall mainly on the rich. But the 1981 Tax Act

essentially abolished them for nearly all Americans, thereby increasing the overall regressivity of the system as well as perpetuating inequality by preserving large fortunes intact.

Federal excise taxes are levied on alcohol, gasoline, tobacco, and telephone calls—goods and services upon which low income citizens spend a much larger proportion of their money than the rich do.

In 1981, the shift toward regressivity became more extreme. The three-step tax cut proposed by the Reagan Administration and passed with few modifications by Congress, along with the reduction in the marginal tax rate on income from 70 percent to 50 percent and the new accelerated depreciation formulas has significantly reduced the progressivity of the income tax.

Conclusion

The net effect of all these tax changes is disputed. At the beginning of the decade, proponents could say that the federal tax system was slightly progressive. Recent tax facts point in another direction. The trend—considering the growth of social security taxes, the decline of progressive taxes like corporate taxes and estate and gift taxes—is towards increasing regressivity.

Increasing regressivity means two things of importance to our analysis. In the first place, it puts a greater burden on low and middle income persons, because regressivity means that those with lower incomes pay higher rates than they would if the system were progressive. Secondly, it means that the middle class bears the burden of the tax system, and therefore of much of life in the United States.

A good way of appreciating the excessive taxation of American wage earners is to compare the total load with the tax burden on an average production worker in different nations. According to Robert Kuttner,[13] in 1974 only three of the seventeen major industrial nations had lower overall tax loads than the United States, yet we ranked eighth in the tax burden on an average production worker. And these comparisons understate the regressivity, because in most of Europe the taxpayer gets more back in free health care and generous family allowances.

The argument becomes even more urgent when one looks at the total tax picture, i.e., federal, state and local taxes. According to data that itself is dated, the total effect of almost all taxes is proportional.

Using the most regressive assumptions about the tax system, Okner and Pechman[14] discovered the system took about 26 percent at most levels, with slightly higher and lower rates at both ends. Under the most progressive assumptions, the rates rose at the upper end of the income scale. But for the vast majority of Americans, with all but the top 1 or 1 percent of incomes, the rates were very nearly proportional.

The point is that in 1966, the system was at best proportional—the same percentage was extracted from everyone's income. Since that time, as shown above, the progressive taxes have been cut back for a variety of reasons and the regressive taxes have increased sharply. The compelling conclusion is that the tax system is regressive. Since it is the middle class who have experienced the largest distortion in their taxes, it is the middle class who bears the burden of the tax system.

[1]See John M. Berry, "Burden in U.S. Not Excessive by World Standards," *The Washington Post* (February 27, 1983), F. 3.

[2]See Berry, F2.

[3]See Harstad, p. 1096.

[4]Harstad, p. 1096.

[5]Otto Friedrich, "Cheating by the Millions," *Time Magazine,* 122(1983), p. 27.

[6]See Friedrich, pp. 27-28.

[7]See Freidrich, p. 28.

[8]Joseph J. Minarik, "Who Doesn't Bear the Tax Burden," in *The Economics of Taxation,* ed. by. Henry J. Aaron and Michael J. Boskin (Washington, D.C.: Brookings Institution, 1980), p. 59.

[9]See *Tax Notes* (July 30, 1984), p. 506. The percentage increase in number of households in this bracket should not be construed as an increase in net worth. "Bracket creep" due to increases in inflation is a major component of the change in numbers.

[10]Gregg A. Esenwein, "A Comparison of Three Personal Tax Cut Proposals: The Reagan, Carter and Senate Finance Committee Proposals," in *Studies in Taxation, Public Finance and Related Subjects, Volume 5* (Washington, D.C.: Fund for Public Policy Research, 1981), p. 45.

[11]Harvey Galper, "Tax Policy," in *Setting National Priorities: The 1984 Budget.* (Washington, D.C.: The Brookings Institution, 1983), p. 174. The table is based on data given on that page.

[12]Thomas B. Edsall, "Recent Revisions Benefit the Rich Relatively More," *The Washington Post* (February 27, 1983), p. F5. The chart is based on data given on page F1.

[13]Robert Kuttner, *The Economic Illusion,* p. 190.

[14]Okner and Pechman, p. 64.

The hardest thing to understand in the world is the income tax.

Albert Einstein

Chapter 6:
The Personal Income Tax
(A Case of Declining Progressivity)

The individual income tax is the largest source of federal revenues. It yielded $328 billion in 1984. The next largest source of government revenues, social insurance taxes, produced $271 billion.

Taxing income as a way of raising government revenue is a relatively recent development in this country. Income, taxed briefly during the Civil War, was not taxed again until 1913 when it became a national institution through the ratification of the Sixteenth Amendment to the Constitution. The individual income tax in America has always had graduated rates. Other countries, notably Great Britain, have had flat-rate personal income taxes.

In 1913, less than 1 percent of the population had to pay the tax, and it drew on only one tenth of one percent of personal income. During World War II, it began to balloon. By 1945 about 75 percent of the population had to pay it; and it was 10 percent of all personal income. Since World War II, this tax reached a high of 12 percent of personal income only in 1969 and again in 1981. During most of the other post-World War II years, it has hovered at about 10 percent of personal income, adjustments being made through changes in the tax law.[1]

In a debate within which there is very little unanimity, there is general agreement about this facet of the federal tax system: the personal income tax is the most progressive in the system. But, with that said, there are still a number of problems. They have to do with vertical equity, horizontal equity, the top limit on marginal rates, the effective rates Americans pay, and the impact of inflation on the tax rate. The rest of this chapter will be devoted to a discussion of these issues.

Vertical Equity

We can best begin our discussion by looking at the statutory rates, the rates that are created by law, the rates we think we pay before we apply deductions, exemptions, credits, loopholes, etc. The following table gives the statutory rates.[2]

TABLE 1: Tax Rate Schedule for Single Individuals, After 1983

If Taxable Income Range is	Pay	+ % on the Excess
$ 0- 2,300	$ 0	0
2,300- 3,400	0	11
3,400- 4,400	121	12
4,400- 6,500	241	14
6,500- 8,500	535	15
8,500- 10,800	835	16
10,800- 12,900	1,203	18
12,900- 15,000	1,581	20
15,000- 18,200	2,001	23
18,200- 23,500	2,737	26
23,500- 28,800	4,115	30
28,800- 34,100	5,705	34
34,100- 41,500	7,507	38
41,500- 55,300	10,319	42
55,300- 81,800	16,115	48
81,800 and over	28,835	50

SOURCE: *U.S. Tax Code,* 1984

One equity issue tax economists apply to the system is vertical equity (another is horizontal equity, which will be discussed below). Vertical equity measures the difference between the rungs of the tax rate ladder and asks if the difference is fair. Does the rate increase fairly from one level to the next? Technically vertical equity measures the difference in tax liability between higher and lower earning taxpayers.

The table indicates that vertical equity is nominal. These official rates increase most rapidly for middle income individuals, and not at all for upper income individuals (above $81,800). Vertical equity would require the increase to take place continuously, and more rapidly as the income scale rises.

The Debate Over Marginal Rates

Most taxpayers are aware that what is expressed in the table above are marginal rates. These rates are the subject of a great deal of debate, particularly about their top levels.

A person's marginal rate is the rate that would apply to his/her last dollar or next to last dollar of income. Suppose Mr. Ashley received $200,000 annual income. If he earned his income in special ways, he would not have to pay taxes on all of it.[3] As a result of exemptions, his taxable income might be reduced to $85,000. Referring to the table on statutory rates, his tax picture would look like this: He would pay nothing on the first $2,300, 12 percent on the next $1,100, 14 percent on the nest $1,000, and so on to 50 percent on the last $3,200.

These figures are already computed in the tables. Since his taxable income is $85,000, Mr. Ashley, in 1984, would pay $28,835 on the first $81,800. On the balance ($3,200-$85,000-$81,800), he would only pay 50 percent or $1,600. His total tax would be $30,435 on a salary of $200,000.

Most of the debate over marginal rates (in this case, that portion upon which Mr. Ashley has to pay 50 percent) has to do with this question: Are marginal rates a disincentive to work or investment? For example, since he is in the 50 percent tax bracket, if Mr. Ashley were considering an overtime assignment for $1000, his after-tax reward would be only $500. Or, if he invests in a security with a ten percent return, the after-tax return would be only five percent. High marginal rates may affect the decision to work overtime or invest. The rationale we have all heard at one time or another is this: Why should I work all those extra hours just to give it to the government?

Economists agree that high marginal rates can affect labor and investment decisions and behavior. But they differ in their analysis of the extent of that impact. Pointing to other countries, they show that high marginal rates discourage neither work nor investment decisions extensively, that power and status are potent factors motivating the acquisition of income and wealth. There is probably a threshhold above which marginal rates would be simply too high. We do not know what that is. There are alternative ways of dealing with the tax system equitably without excessively high marginal rates. These approaches will be considered in chapter ten.

Effective Tax Rates

When figuring Mr. Ashley's taxes above, we neglected to find out what his real or effective tax rate was. We calculated that he paid $30,435 in taxes. Just what percentage of his gross income ($200,000) was that? Dividing the $30,435 by $200,000 yields 15.2 percent. This is Mr. Ashley's effective tax rate, that portion of his gross income that he finally paid the government in taxes. The following table gives the effective rates or the actual rates paid.[4]

TABLE 2: Effective Income Tax Rates for a Family of Four, 1981

Income Level	Effective Income Tax Rate
$ 5,670	-8.82%
8,505	- .51
11,340	4.84
14,175	7.24
17,010	9.06
19,845	10.62
22,680	10.14
25,515	11.26
28,350	12.36
34,020	14.22
39,690	15.32
45,360	16.84
51,030	18.52
56,700	19.80
85,050	25.08
113,400	27.99
226,800	32.90
396,900	32.85
567,000	31.50

SOURCE: Congressional Research Service, 1982

These figures indicate that effective taxes are not as progressive as the statutory rates. Striking is the fact that the effective tax rate exceeds 30 percent only above $200,000 and that it actually declines for gross incomes above $300,000.

The movement of effective rates towards regressivity at the upper end results from the fact that the rich receive and spend their money in ways that can take better advantage of the tax laws. If you earn $12,000 as a factory worker, all your tax is withheld. You have no business deductions to claim, such as those which can be so easily claimed by the rich. If, on the other hand you were a millionaire, and earned primarily capital income, your tax rate would change dramatically because of the deductions to which you would have access.

Horizontal Equity

It makes sense in economic ethics that persons in similar economic circumstances should be treated similarly. This is called horizontal equity. If Mr. Ashley and Mr. Bently have the same income, and the same economic situation, it is reasonable that they should pay the same amount of taxes.

The system, however, does not work that way, as the preceding section of effective tax rates suggests. Due to exclusions and deductions, taxpayers with essentially similar incomes can end up paying quite different amounts to the government tax collector. Two suburban families living side by side, with the same number of children of the same age and the same family incomes could pay taxes that differ by a few thousand dollars. This would happen if the income of one family was exclusively from wages and salaries, and the other was from wages and from capital income (which would be taxed at lower capital gains rates rather than ordinary tax rates). Or, if both made the same salary, but one invested part of it to take advantage of certain tax expenditures, while the other did not. The tax system even discriminates among the rich. It especially favors the rich who earn income from owning capital.

The Impact of Inflation

Inflation, the great distorter of wages and prices, also contributes to the regressivity of the individual income tax. It works to increase the tax burden on middle income persons and has its least effect on upper income persons. Congress and past administrations have been able to sand down its rough edges by consistently making tax cuts. These reductions have usually only compensated for inflation. They have not been real tax cuts in the sense that they increased the real purchasing power of American taxpayers.

An example may help to show how inflation affects the American taxpayer. Suppose a family had the following income tax circumstances in 1980.

Gross Income
$15,000

Federal Income Tax
$1,242

After Tax Income
$13,758

Now assume that the inflation rate for 1980 was 10 percent. In order to maintain the same real gross income level that it had in 1980, this family's income would have to be $16,500 in 1981 (10 percent more than it made in 1980). These are the income tax circumstances for 1981:

Gross Income
$16,500

Federal Income Tax
$1,530

After Tax Income
$14,970

It looks as if this family did not do too badly. The increase in after-tax income is just short of $1,200. But those $14,970 are inflated dollars. To find the real after-tax income for 1981, it is necessary to reduce it by ten percent to $13,609. This means that, due to inflation, the purchasing power of the family has been reduced by $148 in one year. This example shows the pernicious aspects of "bracket creep." Inflation not only pushes individuals and families into higher tax brackets, but simultaneously reduces real incomes.

This effect of inflation on real purchasing power is not evenly distributed over the entire income spectrum. Its impact is in fact regressive. It drives up taxes much more for low and middle income persons than those at higher levels, as the following bar graph indicates.[5]

FIGURE 1: The Regressive Impact of "Bracket Creep"

Percentage Increase in Tax Rates from 10-Percent Inflation by Income Group

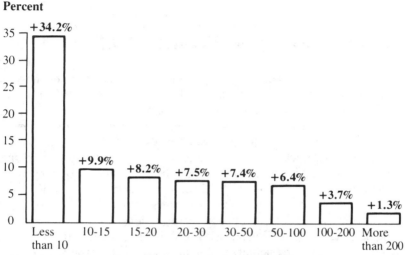

Income figures are in thousands of dollars

SOURCE: Center for Budget and Police Priorities, *Inequity and Decline*, 1983

The reasons for this effect are as follows:[6]

1) In the lower and middle-income range, the tax brackets are closer together than in the upper income ranges. The difference between the 16 percent and 17 percent bracket in 1982 was $2,100, while between the 44 percent and 50 percent bracket it was $7,400. This means that those in the narrower, lower brackets are pushed up into higher brackets at a faster rate than those above them.

2) The tax code limited (in 1982) the tax rate to 50 percent on taxable income over $41,500 (for single individuals). Those that earn over $41,500 experience no increase in their marginal tax rates as a result of inflation-induced wage increases. Each extra dollar of inflation-induced wage and salary income is taxed at the same marginal rate (50 percent) rather than at progressively higher marginal rates. They are not pushed into a higher bracket.

3)   Households that can itemize, i.e., can exclude part of their income from taxes, will not be as adversely affected by inflation as will lower income persons whose income is totally from wage and salary. Since only 40 percent of the income derived from capital gains, for example, is subject to tax, 60 percent of any inflation-induced increase in capital gains is fully exempt from taxation.

The Economic Recovery Tax Act of 1981

With the above as background, we can perhaps better understand the real impact of the Economic Recovery Tax Act of 1981 (ERTA). It was passed by Congress with most of the proposals made by the Reagan Administration intact. Among its major elements were rate reductions: 5 percent in the first year and 10 percent in each of the next two years. Among other significant changes were: a tax deduction for two-earner married couples, and a proposal to index the tax system—to compensate for the effects of inflation—in 1985, decreases in estate and gift taxes, steeply accelerated depreciation schedules, etc. There were also modifications in the corporate income tax provisions.

The personal tax provisions of ERTA represent an across-the-board tax cut. This reduces the tax liabilities of all income groups by the same percentage. This would appear fair, and that is what the designers of the tax package would have us believe. But, ultimately the rich benefit more than the less fortunate from an across-the-board cut. Look at it this way. Ten percent of $12,000 is $1,200, ten percent of $45,000 is $4,500. The result of an across-the-board tax cut is that the rich end up with a larger tax cut.

The break-off point here is $30,000. Families making less than $30,000 will pay a greater share of their income in taxes, ranging from 0.2 percent to 20 percent. Only those making more than $30,000 will receive a tax break, and that becomes significant for those who make more than $100,000 who can expect a net reduction in their taxes of 8 percent. Those with incomes of $200,000 or more can expect reductions of up to 15 percent. The 164,000 persons making more than $200,000 a year will average a tax break of just under $60,000. That is more than the average worker will earn in the same period.[7]

These figures suggest a couple of things. One is that the tax policies put in place by the Reagan Administration favor the rich. A second and more important consequence is that across-the-board tax cuts are unfair. In an ideal world—where the pre-tax distribution of income and wealth were just—with an ideal tax system—one that would tax all persons according to the benefits they receive from the society—this approach to reducing tax burdens would make sense. However, since the system is already unbalanced in favor of higher income earners, across-the-board cuts leave the injustices intact.

Under a progressive tax system, the only way to adopt a tax cut that increases the after-tax income of all groups by the same percentage would be to reduce the tax liabilities by a smaller percentage as one goes up the income scale. This is necessary to compensate for the impact of inflation and rises in payroll and other regressive taxes.

Conclusion

The individual income tax is almost the last remnant of progressivity in the federal tax system, and, in its purest form, is probably the best tax ever devised. But there are some equity questions involved even here. Vertical equity is in short supply, horizontal equity is underminded by loopholes, top marginal rates are being constantly lowered, and effective rates are proportionally lower for persons in higher brackets than those in lower brackets.

The distortions caused by these inequities become evident when the cleaver of across-the-board cuts are applied to the personal income tax, as the Economic Recovery Act of 1981 did. The benefits reaped from this "apparently" fair technique redounded to those in the top brackets, and hardly at all to most other tax payers.

The type of improvement in the individual income tax required by equity is to broaden the base and lower the rates.

---

[1]Richard Goode, *The Individual Income Tax* (Washington, D.C.: The Brookings Institution, 1976), p. 4. Statistics for later years were not available at the time of writing.

[2]Source: *U.S. Tax Code*, 1984.

[3]Exemptions might include capital gains exclusions.

[4]Table based on figures given by Gregg A. Esenwein, "An Analysis of the Impact of the Administration's Proposed Reduction in Personal Income Tax Rates on Typical Taxpayers," *Studies in Taxation, Public Finance and Related Subjects, Volume 5* (Washington, D.C.: Fund for Public Policy Research, 1981), p. 37.

[5]This figure is taken from Robert S. McIntrye and Dean C. Tipps, *Inequity and Decline: How the Reagan Tax Policies Are Affecting the American Taxpayer and the Economy* (Washington, D.C.: Center on Budget and Policy Priorities, 1983), p. 11.

[6]See Gregg A. Esenwein, "The Impact of Inflation and Social Security Tax Increases on the Tax Liabilities of Typical Households," *Studies in Taxation, Public Finance and Related Subjects, Volume 5* (Washington, D.C.: Fund for Public Policy Research, 1981), p. 76.

[7]These figures were taken from McIntyre and Tipps, pp. 22-23.

*Millions of Americans now pay signifi-
cantly higher social insurance taxes than
income taxes.*

Federal Budget, FY 1978

Chapter 7:
Corporation and Social Security Taxes
(Regressivity on the Rise)

Popular images of the corporation deviate sharply from the reality. We tend to think of them as controlled by thousands of small stockholders who elect a board of directors at a general meeting. In this scenario, the board is responsible to the stockholders. One need only go to an annual stockholders meeting to be disabused of this perception of corporate organization.

In reality, 5 percent of the population own 66 percent of the corporate stock, and control most of corporate activity. The rest of the stockholders are too scattered to make much of a difference. In the annual stockholder meetings, the management uses the proxies of the stockholders to vote themselves back into office.

What Is the Corporation Income Tax?

The corporation is a legal entity. By law, it must pay tax on its income, i.e., profits. This tax is calculated in a way similar to the individual income tax, but according to a different rate structure. Here again, the tax is not on gross income, but taxable income which is gross income minus ordinary and special deductions. A corporation, for example, that had a taxable income of $130,000 in 1982 would pay $40,050 in taxes. Its gross profits, however, could have been over $1,000,000.

The corporate income tax was established in 1909 as a one percent tax on corporate profits in excess of $5,000. It rose dramatically, reaching a maximum marginal rate of 52 percent in 1950. Slow economic growth in the 1950's led Congress to give into pressure for special tax incentives. Special exemptions and reductions were put into effect in the 1960's. [1] The impact of these changes has been dramatic. Taxes paid by the nation's corporations dropped to nearly 8.1 percent in 1983.

A study of corporate tax rates by the Joint Committee on Taxation came up with the following corporate tax facts:[2]

• American corporations in 1982 paid an average effective rate of 16.1 percent on income earned within the United States and a foreign tax rate of 55 percent;

• Some industries paid no taxes at all and received refunds. The chemicals industry paid the lowest effective rate with a negative 17.7 percent followed by the insurance industry, financial institutions and aerospace.

• Industries paying the highest effect rates were the rubber industry with 39 percent followed by (in descending order) trucking, tobacco, paper and wood, and wholesalers.

These facts point to startling discrepancies in the corporate tax. While some industries pay a fairly heavy income tax, others, such as financial institutions (including many of the largest banks) pay no U.S. income tax. There does not appear to be any rhyme or reason to the discrepancies. The mix of those paying no taxes are like apples and oranges. It is the same with those paying the highest taxes. The reasons for these peculiarities seems to be skillful lobbying by some companies, and the way complex laws can be made to apply to specific cases.

The Corporation Tax and Total Receipts

Using slightly different figures than those given above, Robert McIntyre and Dean Tipps developed the following picture of the structure of federal tax receipts.[3]

As the graph indicates, while corporate federal receipts dropped nearly 22 percent since 1950, combined personal and social security taxes rose 28 percent as a percentage of total federal government receipts. During that same period that progressive corporate rates declined, progressive personal income taxes increased 10 percent of total government receipts and regressive social insurance taxes increased by 21 percent. It appears that the decline in the effective rate of the federal corporate income tax has contributed to the reduced contribution of this tax to total federal receipts.

Although some of the reductions are from changes in the tax rates, most result from shrinking the definition of the tax base to which the rates are

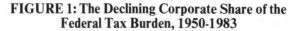

FIGURE 1: The Declining Corporate Share of the Federal Tax Burden, 1950-1983

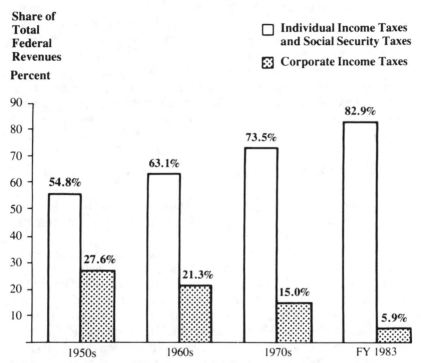

SOURCE: Center for Budget and Policy Priorities, *Inequity and Decline,* 1983

applied. An example of what this means is the ACRS, the change in allowable business depreciation.

The Accelerated Cost Recovery System (ACRS) was a part of the Economic Recovery Tax Act of 1981. It is basically a 15-10-5-3 formula for grouping business assets to determine depreciation deductions. Theoretically, depreciation is an allowance for the decline in value of machines and structures as they age. It is a tax deduction. Here is an example of how it works. Suppose you bought a small warehouse for $100,000. ACRS would allow you to deduct that amount over 15 years. The deduction in the first year would be $12,000; in the second $10,000; in the third $9,000 and so on until the 15th year when the final deduction would be $5,000. These deductions are allowable independently of the economic value of the building, i.e. , regardless of whether the building would have a useful life of 20 or 30 or 50 years, and regardless of whether the real value of the building goes up or down.

Under this formula, autos and light trucks, for example, were assigned a three-year write-off period, other machinery and equipment a five-year period, and structures a ten-year period. These write-offs are considerably shorter than those allowed under earlier legislation. The impact of this formula is startling. The more substantial the allowance, the smaller the percentage of corporate earnings subject to taxes. At an 8 percent annual rate of inflation, it will yield, optimistically, an effective corporate tax rate decline on plant and equipment of 22 percent by 1986, when it is fully phased in.[4]

Who Pays the Corporate Tax?

The corporate income tax has been a subject of controversy for years. Some of the criticism of it has to do with its effect on corporate investments. These will be discussed in chapter nine.

Another point of the controversy, the one that concerns us here, is over the incidence of the tax. Who ultimately pays? Is it a double tax?

Some critics think it is. They claim that it taxes the owners of corporations twice on the income earned by their companies. They are taxed once when the corporation pays its income tax to the government, which deprives the stockholders of some income that would otherwise go to them. And corporate stockholders are taxed again on the dividends they receive.

Unfortunately there is something missing in these calculations. The corporation can choose not to distribute all its earnings to its stockholders. It can decide to reinvest them to raise the value of the stock. These earnings then can compound, untaxed, until the stockholder takes her/his profit by selling the stock. The tax on that profit would be at the capital gains rate, which is currently a good deal less than the rate on ordinary income.

So, who pays the corporate tax? The stockholder? Probably not. Most economists agree that some shifting of the burden occurs, that some portion of the tax is payed either by the worker in the form of lower wages, or the consumer in the form of higher prices. It makes a great deal of difference what sort of shifting occurs, if any, to measure the progressivity of the system. Depending on who bears the corporate tax burden, the tax would be regressive or progressive. Testing various assumptions, Pechman determined that the corporation tax is progressive if it is borne entirely by stockholders, but regressive under other assumptions.[5]

The corporate income tax has strong advocates for its repeal. The issue is becoming rapidly academic as the corporate tax, under present rules, continues, like the Cheshire Cat, to disappear. Soon all that will be left is the smile. Americans, however, need to be concerned about this.

The corporate tax structures in some of our industrial partners is instructive. In 1983, Japan raised 27.8 percent of its federal revenues from corporation taxes; in the U.S., the figure was 6.2 percent. Japan has a very narrow system of corporate deductions, amounting to 2.7 cents for every dollar in corporate taxes, compared to $1.67 for every dollar paid in the U.S. The effective corporate rate in Japan was more than 50 percent.[6]

The British, who like the U.S. have a history of greater and greater corporate tax concessions, have recently changed their tax incentive tune. The conservative Thatcher government, with its pro-business bias, has begun to repeal most of Britian's corporate loopholes.[7]

Were the corporate income tax repealed, the corporate sector could be used to shelter income of high income individuals. In the absence of a tax, income retained by the corporation would be taxed only when realized as a capital gain, and then at lower rates than other types of income.

Americans also need to be concerned about the present state of the corporate tax. It is so structured that many corporations do not pay any tax, and receive refunds from the government.   Ordinary taxpayers are left paying the taxes avoided by these corporations with powerful lobbies. These average taxpayers also bear the brunt of the economic losses caused by deficits and tax-induced inefficiencies.

Social Security Taxes

The collection of payroll taxes began in 1937, two years after the law was passed. The United States was one of the last of the industrialized nations to establish an age-old benefit system. Bismarck created the first such program in Germany in the 1880's. Other European countries quickly followed suit.[8] America's late arrival on the scene should not be surprising. America has always been slower to help the needy than other industrial countries. While Europeans felt it was a nation's responsibility to look after people who had worked all their lives, the American daughters and sons of those same Europeans left old people to look after themselves. They were expected to pay for their retirement out of their own savings. Failing that, it was up to their children to support them. Private charity and minimal government relief programs were the last resort.

None of these solutions were workable during the Depression. Retirement savings were wiped out. Unemployment made it impossible for children to support their aged parents. Franklin Roosevelt responded to this situation characteristically: he created the Social Security System in 1935.

The system began with a tax rate on employee and employer each of 1 percent. The wage base was $3,000; the maximum tax paid, $30. The earnings base was increased in 1951 for the first time to $3,600 annually, and self-employed persons were included for the first time. Coupled with many expansions and amendments to the system, more than a dozen changes have been made since the early 1950's. In 1981, employer and employee were each paying 6.65 percent, and the wage base was $29,700. In that year, the maximum paid was $1,975.05.[9]

The growth of the social security or payroll taxes has been severe, and has to do with some political realities. Social security taxes are easy for Congress and the administration to raise because of the link people perceive between the tax and the benefit they receive. Income taxes turn out to be highly unpopular taxes, perhaps because taxpayers do not necessarily perceive a similar linkage. The popular move for politicians seeking re-election is to cut these taxes whenever feasible. In addition, corporation taxes have declined because of the successful lobbying efforts of the business community.

The "link" between the payroll tax and social security benefits is often misunderstood by the taxpayer.[10] Social security is a pay-as-you-go system. It is not an insurance system. The taxes withdrawn from a worker's check provide benefits for those who are currently retired. The money is not an insurance premium for the worker's own future benefits. The money is not sitting in a bank waiting for the worker to retire. Since social security is basically a cash-in, cash-out system, the money collected from any generation of workers is used to pay the benefits of the concurrent generation of retirees. The linkage is fundamental to the system. It gives workers a putative right to retirement benefits because they paid into the system during their working years. By collecting the payroll tax, the government obligates itself to maintain a system to assure workers of benefits they had been promised.

Social security planners understood from the very beginning that the system would probably become too expensive to be supported solely by a payroll tax. They expected that the tax would become too burdensome for employees by around 1965, when they would have to pay about 2.5 percent. When that occurred, it was their recommendation that general revenue funds be used to support the system. That point was reached in 1959, however, and no such adjustment was made.

The tax burden has increased. It now comes to 7.05 percent and is on the rise. The increases have been due to the addition of disability and health programs, and the increase in longevity. President Reagan appointed a committee to study the possibilities of meeting long and short term obligations in social security benefits, when bankruptcy threatened the system. The committee came up with some short term solutions, but was unable to face the long term problem, which is how to finance the retirement of the baby boom generation in the next century.

Incidence and Regressivity

When the payroll tax was designed, half the tax was levied on the employer and half on the employee. The obvious intention was to divide the burden. Most economists, however, believe that the entire tax is borne by the employee. They base their claims on complicated analyses, but conclude that the employer extracts her/his portion of the payroll tax from the worker in reduced wages. Some economists believe the consumer pays the employer share in higher prices in the market place. Economists generally agree that it is not the employer who bears his/her intended burden of the tax.

There is relatively little difference in impact between these two assumptions. Under one or the other, the payroll tax proves to be very regressive, as has been demonstrated repeatedly.[11] The tax is greatest on those we would call middle class, and lowest on the very rich. A recent analysis indicates that the trend has remained the same since the 1966 data used by Pechman and Okner. It showed that the change in effective social security rates affect most drastically those in the $20,000-$50,000 income bracket, and least drastically those with incomes over $100,000.[12] There are two causes for the regressivity of the payroll tax. In the first place it is levied only on wage income. Excluded is all income from capital, which becomes a greater source of economic well-being as income increases.

A close look at the figures shows how these factors contribute to regressivity. In 1985, the payroll tax rate is 7.05 percent on a taxable base of $39,600. This means that the tax applies to only the first $39,600 of wages The following table shows the amount and percentage of income paid by each income level.

No matter what the income, the amount paid remains constant after the maximum of $39,600 is reached. But as income increases, the percentage of income decreases sharply.

Since social security is a pay-as-you-go system, and since the employer's share is shifted either to the worker or the consumer, this table makes it evident that it is the working class that is supporting the retired workers.

TABLE 1: Social Security Taxes as a Percentage of Income

Income Level	Amount Paid	Percentage Of Income
$ 10,000	$ 705	7.05%
20,000	1410	7.05
30,000	2115	7.05
39,600	2792	7.05
40,000	2792	6.98
50,000	2792	5.58
100,000	2792	2.79
200,000	2792	1.39
300,000	2792	0.93
500,000	2792	0.56

Almost none of the payments for social security come from the rich, as would be the case if the funds came from general revenues, which are supported by the more progressive income taxes.

The fact that all wages above a maximum ($39,600 in 1985) are excluded is the second cause of the regressivity of the social security payroll tax. This means that most of the income of high salaried persons are not factored in. It also means that no exemptions are included for number of dependents, medical expenses, casualty loss. As a flat tax, it does not measure, or allow for differences, in ability-to-pay.

Some financing problems plagued social security in the early 1980's. The Reagan Administration took some steps to meet the short term financial problems. The major change was an adjustment in the automatic cost of living increases, which was delayed for six months.

That proposal seems minimal on a per capita basis, since it would reduce benefits an average of $110 per person. It is estimated to save $22.4 billion over a five year period.[13] The proposal does nothing to alter the regressivity of the system. It is in fact anti-progressive since it basically affects the working class, with little or no impact on the upper class.

There are alternate ways of adjusting for social security financing problems. European countries, which have a better record than the United States in social security expenditures, have had similar financing problems.

Steps they have taken to increase revenues include the removal of ceilings on payroll contributions, increasing the payroll tax rates for the self-employed, interfund transfers, special excise-type taxes and supplements from general revenue.[14] While not all of these are progressive methods of dealing with the system, it needs to be noted that all the European countries supplement their social security funds from general revenue.

Conclusion

While trying to figure out who really pays the corporation tax is complex, it is evident that without it much income and wealth could be sheltered. Lacking a corporation tax, a substantial part of the individual income tax would be permanently lost through retention of earnings by corporations.

Economic arguments against the corporation tax hold hardly any water. There is no evidence that it has impaired the growth of the corporate sector. Major tasks are to eliminate the continual seeping away of the corporation tax, and to eliminate the large differences in effective rates of different corporations.

The programs the payroll tax pays for—social security, unemployment compensation, hospital and medical care for retired workers—are good and needed. But the taxes used to finance these programs are regressive, and shifted downward from employer to employee to consumer.

Increases in payroll taxes also have a major deleterious effect on the progressivity of the tax system. Equity solutions to these problems would be removal of the maximum taxable ceiling, integration of the payroll and income taxes and use of general funds for future financing of social security benefits.

.

---

[1]This data, with an informative graph of historical corporate rates, can be found in Charles R. Hulten and June A. O'Neill, "Tax Policy," in *The Reagan Experiment* (Washington, D.C.: Urban Institute, 1982), pp. 106-107.

[2]Joint Committee on Taxation, U.S. Congress, *Study of 1982 Effective Tax Rates of Selected Large U.S. Corporations* (Washington, D.C.: U.S. Government Printing Office, 1983), pp. 5-10.

[3]McIntrye and Tipps, p. 100.

[4]Hulten and O'Neill, p. 111.

[5]Joseph A. Pechman, *Federal Tax Policy,* 3rd ed. (Washington, D.C.: Brookings Institution, 1977), pp. 129-36.

[6]Robert S. McIntyre and Robert Folen, *Corporate Income Taxes in the Reagan Years* (Washington, D.C.: Citizens for Tax Justice, 1984), pp. 7-8.

[7]McIntyre and Folen, p. 8.

[8]_____, "Your Stake in the Fight Over Social Security," *Consumer Reports* (September, 1981), p. 503.

[9]For a history of the social security system, see Alicia H. Munnell, *The Future of Social Security* (Washington, D.C.: Brookings Institution, 1977), p. 155-184.

[10]On the idea of linkage, see *Consumer Reports,* p. 503-504.

[11]See, for example, Okner and Pechman, p. 59.

[12]Gregg A. Esenwein, "The Impact of Inflation. . .", p. 82.

[13]*An Analysis of the President's Budgetary Proposals for Fiscal Year 1984* (Washington, D.C.: Congressional Budget Office, 1983), p. 98.

[14]See *Social Security in Europe: The Impact of an Aging Population.* Senate Special Committee on Aging (Washington, D.C.: Government Printing Office, 1981), pp. 1-2, 13.

In this world nothing is certain but death and taxes.

Benjamin Franklin

It may be that the real certainties of the world are death and tax avoidance.

Professor George Cooper

Chapter 8:
The Real Truth About Tax Loopholes

(On What They Really Are and Who They Favor)

You know them as loopholes, deductions, credits exemptions. The government devised another term, "tax expenditures," for them. It is also the most confusing, because it is, on the surface at least, ambiguous. But, on closer inspection, it makes some sense. It precisely describes the reality. Taxes are a way of collecting money. Expenditures are ways of spending money. A tax expenditure is a way of spending money by not collecting it.

The Congressional Budget Act of 1974 defines tax expenditures as "revenue losses." They result from special exclusions, exemptions or deductions from gross incomes. Exceptions to the normal structure and process of the individual and corporate income tax, they reduce the taxes that particular groups of persons have to pay. The home mortgage interest deduction is an example. If Mr. Ashley deducts $2,000 because of his interest payment, that is a tax expenditure. Normally, he would have to pay 50 percent of that, or $1,000, to Uncle Sam. The tax code allows a particular group of taxpayers—homeowners, in this case—to keep so much of their money.

What the government is doing, in fact, is spending that one thousand dollars on the Mr. Ashley's house. It is saying, "It's my money, but you keep it." The effect of a tax expenditure is to subsidize a particular activity. The home mortgage interest deduction subsidizes home buying. In this sense, it is no different from a budget outlay.

That doesn't sound like much. But tax expenditures measured $365 billion in 1985. A lot of that is money the government could have collected, but did not. The federal government would not exactly collect that amount were it to eliminate all tax expenditures. Some persons might decide, for example, not to participate in a certain activity were it not subject to favorable tax treatment.

We are far from that perfect day when all tax expenditures will be eliminated and one's taxes will be a simple calculation. The trend is in the opposite direction. In 1967 there were 50 items listed in the budget as tax expenditures for a total loss of 136.6 billion. That was about 4.4 percent of the GNP. In 1982, tax expenditures had grown to $253.5 billion—8.4 percent of GNP. They included 104 items.[1]

Those numbers ought to serve as a red flag for most readers. And with good reason, which will be discussed below. First it might help to learn a little more about what tax expenditures are.

Progressivity and Tax Expenditures

The major tax expenditures are:[2]

1) *Personal deductions under the individual income tax.* These include such items as deductions for state and local income taxes, sales and property taxes, charitable contributions, medical expenses, and interest paid.

2) *Exclusions from taxable income.* Among these are state and local government bond interest, employee benefits; also social security, unemployment and welfare payments.

3) *Preferential treatment of long-term capital gains.* Capital gains are the income that results from increases in the value of investments like stocks, bonds, real estate, houses. It is taxed at a rate that is less than half the marginal tax rate that applies to wage and salary income.

4) *Tax credits and accelerated depreciation for investments.* ACRS is an example of this type of tax expenditure.

The reader will not be surprised to hear that tax expenditures are not progressive. They are only for the rich or well-to-do. Tax deductions for individuals provide little benefits to the 69 percent of taxpayers who do not file itemized returns. In 1981, for example, 74 percent of the benefits from the mortgage interest deduction went to the 19 percent of taxpayers with annual incomes exceeding $30,000; and 94.1 percent of the benefits from the exclusion of interest on state and local bonds went to taxpayers with adjusted gross incomes exceeding $50,000.[3]

The preceding figures also suggest that tax expenditures affect the progressivity of the tax system. It should not surprise the reader that they, in fact, do. The following graph illustrates the extent of regressivity introduced into the tax system by tax expenditures.[4]

FIGURE 1: Average Tax Savings per Taxpayer by Income Group

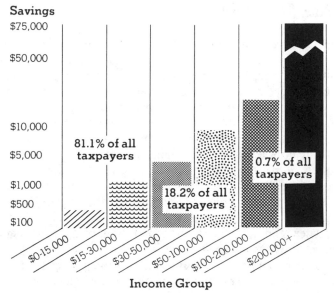

(Not including corporate tax and 19 individual tax preferences not published in Treasury data)

SOURCE: The Taxpayers Committee, 1984

As this graph makes perfectly clear, tax expenditures really benefit only 18.9 percent of all taxpayers. The graph also makes the regressivity of tax expenditures obvious: the higher the income group, the more they reduce taxes. Those in the highest tax bracket receive the greatest advantage.

Most of the tax expenditures for the poor are need related. They come from the exclusions for: social security benefits, veterans benefits, disability

compensation pensions, earned income credit and public assistance benefits. Middle class tax expenditures are consumption related for the most
part. The largest consumption provisions include the deductibility of non-
business state and local taxes, the deductibility of mortgage interest and
property taxes on owner-occupied houses, the deductibility of charitable
contributions and of medical expenses.

The bulk of high income tax expenditures have to do with investment
expenses and income. They include capital gains, depreciation on business
capital and tax-exempt bonds.[5]

What Are Tax Shelters

Tax shelters have been one of the few growth industries in recent years.
While the rest of the economy was in a recession, the number of shelters,
and the number of people taking advantage of tax shelters, grew rapidly.

Because they are not eligible for tax shelters, most Americans have
hardly any idea of how they work. Tax shelters really are games for upper
income Americans only, those in the 50 percent tax bracket, for these
reasons: First of all, the participant must have enough money to make an
initial investment of a few thousand dollars. Secondly, because one of the
primary assets of the shelter comes from being able to deduct the financial
advantages of the shelter from one's taxes. And the best advantage is for
those in the 50 percent bracket. For anyone else, it would not make
financial sense.

A tax shelter is an investment where part or all of the payoff takes the
form of lower taxes. Many shelters creatively assemble various provisions
of the tax code into a package with windfall consequences for those who
take part in the shelter. These artistic creations of high paid tax lawyers are
often called syndicated tax shelters.

Suppose you were to pick up the *Wall Street Journal*, and see an ad for a
tax shelter with an 8 to 1 write-off potential. What would that mean if you
took advantage of it? Well, to begin with, an 8 to 1 write-off potential
means that there is an eight dollar deduction from your gross income for
every dollar you invest.

Let's assume you are in the 50 percent tax bracket. You invest $10,000
in this shelter. For your investment you get $80,000 worth of deductions
in the first year. Now you apply that to your taxes. Because you are in the 50
percent bracket, your deduction is worth $40,000. You can now deduct
$40,000 from your tax bill. For your $10,000 , you end up with $30,000 in

your hand. You made the $30,000 by investing $10,000. And you made it at taxpayers' expense.

How did this happen? How were the shelter syndicators able to offer the 8 to 1 write off? They packaged some of the advantages the tax code offers capital investors. Two basic components of the shelter syndication are up-front loading and leveraging.

Up-front loading amounts to putting all the expenses for the project in the first year, and not getting any taxable income until a later year. The tax code allows immediate deductions for raising cattle, hen's eggs, thorough-bred horses, for growing Christmas trees, for professional sport franchises, for real estate ventures, equipment leases, for oil and gas drilling, equipment leasing and motion picture making. Raising cattle can easily be up-front loaded. There is little capital involved. One does not have to buy buildings or equipment. All the expenses go into feeding and labor. These can be loaded into the first year, and deducted in that year. By the time the investment produces income you will have sold it (at a capital gain) or lined up another shelter to cover that income.

Leveraging is the second component. This is the one that allows the big bucks to be made at Uncle Sam's (read: you the taxpayer) expense. The $70,000 difference between your $10,000 investment in the 8 to 1 shelter and the $80,000 you deduct on your taxes is a loan. The loan is made for you by the syndicate. It handles all the actual cattle transactions, and pays off the loan the following year through the sale of the cattle. For you, it is merely a paper transaction. In essence, you are depreciating the bank's share of the assets. You borrow from the bank—through the syndicate—and depreciate the bank's money. You are at some risk—the cattle could be wiped out by the plague. But even here, there is an extraordinary amount of protections.

The tax advantages do not end here. There are ways of deferring income, paying income at the lower capital gains rate, gifting investments, and so on.

From an ethical perspective, there are two problems with tax shelters. One is that many shelters encourage bad investments. People make money by losing money. A person in a tax shelter makes all his/her money through tax deductions. If the shelter produces income, that person would have to pay taxes on that income. Ultimately it does not matter to the shelterer what the investment is. Our participant could have invested in it without knowing what the business was, just as we were able to explain it without telling you what kind of business was associated with it. It could have been producing eggs, or drilling for oil, or making a spaghetti western.

The second is that the profit from the tax shelter (in the case described above, the $30,000) is payed for by you the taxpayer, simply because that amount is tax money that is taken back by certain taxpayers, legally but nevertheless really. This means that the government has to make other adjustments in its tax raising activities in order to collect the dollars it needs to fund its activities.[6]

Who Gains from Capital Gains?

Capital gains is the most important item in holding down the taxes of high income persons. The main problem with the existing income tax system is its inability to reach capital income adequately. According to a 1980 Treasury Department study, net capital income in the economy was $305.5 billion. Of that only $96.6 billion was reported on individual income tax returns. Only one-third of all capital income is included in the personal income tax base. The result is the average marginal rate on all capital income is about 10 percent.[7]

How is this all possible?

Capital gains are the profits a person makes on the sale of stocks, bonds, land, buildings and other kinds of property—on capital. If Mr. Ashley buys a share of stock for $100 and sells it for $1000, the capital gain is $900.

If that gain were taxed as part of the normal income tax structure, it would be added to Mr. Ashley's taxable income, and be subject to his marginal rate. Since, however, it is not a wage or salary, but a capital gain, Mr. Ashley can exclude 60 percent of that gain ($540) from his taxable income. He has to pay tax on only $360. If that capital gain were taxed at the top marginal rate, Mr. Ashley's tax would be $450. Instead, it is $180.

Suppose Mr. Bentley earned $1000 in wages and salary by putting in overtime. Mr. Ashley would pay just 40 percent of what Mr. Bentley has to pay in taxes. The anamoly is that much of capital gains finds its source in labor. A person invests in IBM. Because of the work and success of the people at IBM, the stock goes up. The investor gets both the profit and pays less tax than the workers.

To enjoy capital gains, one must own property. This immediately takes many American families out of the picture. The following table gives an idea of the extent distribution of capital gains.[8]

The capital gains tax has been deservedly criticized because only an elite group could benefit from it. It has also been criticized because of the amount of complexity it introduces into the tax system. There are too many of those complexities to go into. But there is one that turns out to be

TABLE 1: Composition of 1980 Income

Adjusted Gross Income Level	Wage & Salary Income as % of total money income	Capital Gains as % of total money income
$ 30,000- 50,000	96.13%	3.87%
50,000-100,000	91.47	8.53
100,000-200,000	86.85	13.15
200,000-500,000	76.26	23.74
greater than 500,000	67.05	32.95

SOURCE: Department of the Treasury, Internal Revenue Service, 1982

an especially large windfall for the taxpayer who has a capital gain. It has to do with unrealized appreciation at death.

In the first place, you need to know that a capital gain is not taxed until it is realized. Some lucky people bought homes in central cities in 1976 for $25,000, and found those homes worth, through no fault of their own, $100,000 in 1980. Mr. Ashley was one of them. In the four years his house had appreciated $75,000—i.e., by 1980, it was worth $75,000 more than when he purchased it. So long as he does not sell the house, he has an unrealized capital gain of $75,000. As long as it is unrealized, it is not taxed. If he were to sell the house in 1980, then he would pay taxes on the $75,000, not at the regular rate, but at the more modest capital gains rate of 40 percent.

Suppose that poor Mr. Ashley died in 1984, left the house, now worth $150,000 to his wife. The unrealized capital gain would now be $125,000. His wife could sell it in full and pay no capital gains at all. The tax law puts on its myopia glasses, and recognizes only the price of the house when she inherited it. The unrealized capital gains is "forgotten," and the tax on it forever lost to the American people. This is, of course, how a great deal of wealth is handed down from one generation to another. Millions of dollars are passed along as unrealized capital gains and never taxed.

Capital gains preferences need to be objected to on many grounds.

• Horizontal equity is violated because investors with capital gains are taxed more lightly than taxpayers with equivalent incomes derived from different sources.

• Most of the benefit of capital gains is realized by upper-income individuals (in 1983, 60 percent of the savings went to taxpayers with more than $100,000 of reported income), thereby reducing the progressivity of the federal income tax system.

• Many private resources of the country are devoted to tax minimization when they could be devoted to other pursuits.

The arguments in favor of the capital gains tax and other tax expenditures will be discussed more fully in the next chapter. At this point, however, it should be noted that the above arguments hold the most weight for the author of this book.

Conclusion

It is obvious that tax loopholes are benefits for high-income and wealthy taxpayers. Every year the government loses billions of dollars in potential revenue because of them. These loopholes have two effects: they cause people in the same economic circumstances to be treated differently—some paying higher taxes, some lower; and they allow the wealthy to avoid a great deal of taxation.

Tax shelters are really investments, not in the economy, but in the tax system itself. The main benefits to shelterers are not from their investment in cattle or oil or egg production, but from the return they receive in tax deductions. The ethical problem: tax shelters encourage bad investments, and they force other taxpayers to pay the return that the shelterer receives.

The main problem with the existing income tax system is its inability to reach capital gains adequately. Only one-third of all capital income is included in the personal income tax base. From the standpoint of equity, capital gains should be fully taken into account in determining individual tax liability.

---

[1]*Tax Expenditures: Budget Control Options and Five-Year Budget Projections for Fiscal Years 1983-1987* (Washington, D.C.: Congressional Budget Office, 1982), pp. 11-13.
[2]This categorization is based on Joseph J. Minarik, "Tax Expenditures," in *Setting National Priorities: The 1982 Budget* (Washington, D.C. Brookings Institution, 1981), p. 272. Other breakdowns are available, depending on the information the author wishes to display.
[3]Ruth Simon, "Radical Tax Reform," *New York Times* (February 28, 1982).

⁴This graph has been supplied by the Taxpayers Committee.

⁵Nonna A. Nota, "Tax Expenditures: The Link Between Economic Intent and the Distribution of Benefits Among High, Middle, and Low Income Groups," *Studies in Taxation, Public Finance and Related Subjects, Vol. 6* (Washington, D.C.: The Fund for Public Policy Research, 1981), pp. 61-64.

⁶The example given here was based on elements of various tax shelters described by James J. Cramer, "Tax Shelter Wizard," *Harper's,* 266 (April, 1983), pp. 20-27; Emanuel S. Burstein, "Syndicated Tax Shelters: A Survey of the Issues," *Studies in Taxation, Public Finance and Related Subjects, Volume 6* (Washington, D.C.: Fund For Public Policy Research, 1982), pp. 3-22.

⁷Eugene Steuerle, "Is Income from Capital Subject to Individual Income Taxation?" *Office of Tax Analysis Paper 42* (Washington, D.C.: Department of the Treasury, 1980), pp. 9, 12.

⁸Gregg A. Esenwein, "An Analysis of the Impact of the Administration's Proposed Reduction. . . ," p. 28.

Tax incentives haven't helped us one damn bit.

Firestone Chairman John J. Nevins

Chapter 9:
Tax Expenditures and Economics
(On the Effect of Taxes on Economic Growth)

Why do we have tax expenditures, anyway? The principal reason is for what Robert Kuttner has wisely called the "capital formation theology." According to this theology, "the most effective way to stimulate investment is to increase the after-tax return on investment. In other words, make investment more profitable by lightening the tax load on wealthy investors."[1]

The significant point here is that the theory operates like a theology. It is part of a value system, namely the free market ideology, for which there is hardly any empirical basis. There has been a tremendous amount of literature on the topic. A survey that originated in the Congressional Research Service concluded: "There is little evidence from either economic theory or empirical analyses that higher rates of return—such as those offered by tax expenditures—actually increase the rate of savings in the economy."[2]

There is little evidence that it is true, yet "capital formation" continues to act as a symbol in government fiscal policy. The term is more expressive of a certain set of beliefs than it is substantive with economic content.

In the U.S. at the present time, the dominant economic theory is that renewed vigor requires a smaller public sector and a redistribution of tax load to decrease the share paid by corporations and upper income individuals. It does not have to be that way. Many of our western industrial partners have demonstrated that capital formation, in the sense of increasing the net investment of plant and equipment, can be maintained or increased in a manner consistent with distributional goals.

First, you need to be aware that the supply of savings in the economy is by definition equal to the amount of investment. Then the issue becomes how to increase savings. The approach in the U.S. has been to use tax incentives.

On the other hand, "The German government," according to Kuttner, "has adopted subsidy policies intended to promote savings by moderate income households. Households may contract with the government to contribute to seven-year blocked savings accounts. At the end of the period, they may withdraw the funds, receive a government bonus, and apply the proceeds to the down-payment on a house. In addition, they receive a mortgage at a preferential rate."[3]

The plan combines a social goal—home ownership—with an economic one—increased savings. The plan broadens the distribution of wealth by 1) subsidizing savings made by moderate income households, and 2) bringing homeownership within the reach of additional moderate income families. As it does this, it increases the pool of savings.[4]

Contrast this plan with the "All Savers" tax incentive of our 1981 Economic Recovery Tax Act, which cost the government billions of dollars. The incentive benefitted those who were in the 30 percent or higher tax bracket, so it was very regressive. Its impact on savings was insignificant as most savers merely shifted their assets from one savings account to another.

The debate over capital formation is ultimately one of quantity versus quality. The question is: To what extent are our economic problems caused by an inadequate quantity of capital investment and poor allocation of capital?

Since it is represented by one of the strongest corporate and business lobbies in Washington, DC, the idea of capital formation merits some discussion. Its advocates are simply saying that capital (machinery, plants, stock, land) needs to be taxed lightly to encourage investment—which is precisely what capital gains, ACRS and many of the other tax expenditures are intended to do. But there is no clear cut case that these expenditures are efficient, i.e., achieve that goal, increase investment.

1. Widely accepted economic studies indicate that only about one-fifth or one-sixth of economic growth is contributed by capital at all. Most of the increase has been due to more efficient allocation of resources, technological breakthrough, rising levels of worker education and the composition of the workforce.[5]

2. There is no capital shortage. Investment as a percentage of GNP has averaged about 9.6 percent since the early 1950's.

3. Despite the free market rhetoric, business is not the best allocator of money. During the booming post-wars years, Detroit invested its capital in style and not efficiency; Penn Central's profit went into real estate and not modernization; steel companies invested capital in chemical industries

rather than plant modernization.

4. The business of business is profits. It will invest in areas where it thinks demand exists or can be created, despite the level of after-tax earnings.

5. Many of those industrial countries that have higher taxes on capital investment have also had high rates on growth. Both Germany and Japan have high taxes on capital investment. Both have had higher rates of growth than the United States. Britain on the other hand has the most liberal depreciation allowances. It also has Europe's most sluggish economy.[6]

Ultimately, our rate of investment depends on a number of factors. There is no simple correlation between tax level and the fraction of total output that society sets aside to invest. The tax expenditure approach—the capital formation theology—is unnecessary. The case we want to make is that tax expenditures can and should be handled on the expenditure side of the budget.

The Case Against Tax Expenditures

Tax expenditures are conscious decisions on the part of policy makers to reduce the taxes of certain taxpayers. They are not inadvertent defects in our tax system which enable certain taxpayers to slip through, paying little or no taxes. For the most part they are especially enacted to encourage certain economic or social behavior.

The All Savers certificates, and IRA and Keogh Accounts were created to encourage the growth of savings and loan associations and mutual savings banks. The charitable deduction is intended to encourage philanthropy. The campaign contribution deduction and credit is intended to foster a wider participation in political contributions. The ACRS was intended to increase productivity.

In the preceding section of this chapter, we discussed the theory behind tax incentives. We pointed out the limitations of the favorite arguments of the capital formation theologians. Here we would like to address the limitations of tax expenditures themselves.

1. Tax incentives are not free.

When the federal government spends money through various tax expenditures, the amount of resources available for other projects is reduced. This act of fiscal benevolence puts the government on the horns of a dilemma. It is forced either to cut funds for existing programs or to raise everyone's taxes to make up the difference. If one group of taxpayers pays less tax, the rest of the taxpayers will have to pay more.

2. Tax expenditures put a great deal of American income outside the progressive tax structure.

Tax loopholes turn out to be one of our primary growth industries. In 1978 they totaled $89 billion; $322 billion in 1984, and a projected $436 billion in 1987 for an increase of $345 billion, or 490 percent in nine years. These figures represent the amount of income that has been excluded from the tax rolls.

3. Tax expenditures are not subject to close scrutiny or monitoring.

We do not know if they have achieved their objectives, how they have done so, who is using them, how they compare to other means of achieving the same goals. Tax expenditures are likely to remain in operation beyond their useful period of time. They have not been periodically reviewed as are direct expenditures. (Congress, long aware of this problem, is beginning to put time limitations on new tax expenditures.)

4. Many tax incentives pay taxpayers for doing what they would do anyway.

Businesses get ACRS and investment credits on machinery they would have bought routinely to replace worn equipment. A Joint Committee on Taxation study estimated that perhaps 90 percent of the investment tax credit is wasted and only 10 percent additional equipment purchased.[7] The literature on the locational decision of businesses is filled with example after example of the non-effect of tax incentives. Businesses decide on sites for their factories, warehouses and corporate offices on the basis of numerous other factors. In one study by the Joint Economic Committee, tax incentives were fourteenth in a list of fifteen factors which motivate locational decisions.[8]

5. Many tax incentives waste money because of fundamental flaws in design.

The tax exemption for state and local bonds is a classic example. They consistently cost the federal government more in tax losses than states and localities benefit. The loss on the federal level is greater than the gain on the local level.[9]

6. Many tax incentives help the rich rather than the economy.

This is clearly the case for tax shelters. Because of the tax benefits from these shelters, the investments do not have to be economically sound to be profitable to the participating taxpayer. The investment is predicated on losing money to achieve tax benefits for the wealthy.

7. Tax subsidies can encourage the misallocation of resources and distort the normal market mechanism.

Tax incentives are designed to alter the allocation of resources, but we have found out, for example, that ACRS has led to a distortion in the economy, admitted by the presidential administration that installed it, and an emphasis on short-term instead of long-term goals.

Perhaps the most devastating criticisms of tax expenditures have come from two unlikely sources. The first originates with the current British Financial Secretary of the conservative Thatcher government. According to the Secretary "the assumption that tax incentives meant better investment has been proved alarmingly wrong. There are many reasons why the UK (United Kingdom) has made poor use of capital but it is hard to escape the conclusion that a tax regime which subsidized and encouraged projects with low returns has been an important contributing factor."[10]

The second is from the Federal Reserve Board. In its study, *Public Policy and Capital Formation*, it declared: "'. . . This study concludes that the existing capital stock is misallocated, probably seriously . . . primarily because of distortions caused by inflation and U.S. tax laws . . . As a result capital is not applied to its most efficient uses . . . The cost to the nation has been lessened productivity growth and reduced business output."[11]

Tax Incentives and Direct Expenditures

Tax expenditures are supposed to be incentives. They are designed to induce certain types of behavior in response to the monetary benefits available. Is that kind of tax inducement really necessary? After all, direct government expenditures operate in the same way. They support certain types of activities and serve to stimulate that kind of behavior. Federal public housing programs and housing for senior citizens are a clear example of how government expenditures operate to encourage certain types of activity.

In this section we are going to argue that any goal that can be accomplished by a tax expenditure, can also be effected by a direct government expenditure, with many advantages.

Many of the tax expenditures now on the books can be easily converted into direct expenditures. The existing tax incentive for charitable giving could be structured as a direct expenditure: the government would match an individual's contribution to charity with a proportional contribution of its own to the same charity. Tax credits to an employer for employment training could be structured as grants or contract payments to the employer. Tax benefits to the aged can be structured as cash payments to the aged instead of social security exclusions, etc.[12] This kind of restructuring would unmask the irrationality and fundamental unfairness of many of our tax expenditure programs. How equitable does a medical assistance program for the aged look that would cost $200 million, under which $90 million would go to persons with incomes over $50,000 and only $8 million to persons with incomes under $5,000? Or a social security benefit program that would not pay anyone whose income was under $3,300, but would pay benefits of up to 50 percent of imputed taxable income for those whose income were over $100,000? Or a subsidized loan program for housing under which a wealthy person could borrow the funds at 3 percent interest, but a poor person would have to pay 7-8 percent?[13] Well, this is precisely how the tax expenditures for medical expense deductions, social security income benefits exclusions and the five-year amortization of rehabilitation expenditures have operated.

A clear advantage in simple justice to restructuring tax loopholes as direct expenditures is that it would simplify the complexity of the tax system while providing a way to monitor the benefits. Tax expenditures are usually open-ended; they place no limit on how much tax benefit a taxpayer can earn. They are equivalently blank checks to the user. We have no way of knowing how the dollars actually were used or how cost effective the purchase was. Direct expenditures permit close government scrutiny over how the money is spent. And permit it to be monitored carefully. Resort to tax expenditures greatly decreases the ability of the government to maintain control over the management of its priorities. This runs counter to our concern for the ordering of national priorities and the wise allocation of our resources.

Conclusion

We have examined tax loopholes in this chapter, and have found them wanting. "Capital formation" should be a red flag to most taxpayers. It states rather baldly that the tax system should be skewed to the advantage of the rich. It is one more Trojan Horse for trickle-down economics.

The question we asked in this chapter was: is it really true? Are tax expenditures, which favor principally the rich, necessary? The answer we gave was a clear, firm "no." Fairness in the tax system does not have to be sacrificed to economic efficiency. Whatever can be a tax expenditure can be a direct expenditure. Whatever is being done on the tax side of the budget by way of special tax treatment of certain investments can be handled just as well on the outlay side. And it can be done better, and more rationally.

Behind the capital formation theology, and the system of tax loopholes, is an ideology that claims that economic growth requires that the rich and well-to-do receive the benefits from government fiscal policies. This is not necessarily true. In its 1982 *Annual Report*, the Congressional Joint Economic Committee made this rather startling claim on the basis of a careful analysis of major industrial countries:

"Were the 'trickle-down' theory valid, countries with high inequality would show rapid growth, while those with less inequality would be more nearly stagnant. Analysis of the leading industrial democracies not only fails to confirm this high inequality/high growth hypothesis, it shows just the opposite. Those countries with above average inequality have grown less rapidly than the normal more nearly equal countries."[14]

Equality of income, wealth and political power have far more to do with economic growth than a narrow concentration of wealth, or programs that acerbate inequality. It appears that biblical principles of justice for the poor make sense as guidelines for economic and fiscal policies, and as a directive for redesigning the tax system.

A Note of Tax-Exempt Organizations and Charitable Gifts

Since the beginning of the federal income tax, Church entities and similar groups have been exempt from taxation.[15] They were seen as inherently ex-exempt from taxation because the contributions of their membership are the mutual benefit of the members themselves or of those in need. Under this rationale, these groups did not truly earn income in the usual sense meant by the code. Another important rationale is that these groups perform services in society that government itself would otherwise have to perform.

Not only are the very existence and operation of these organizations encouraged by the Code, but the taxpaying public is encouraged to support them by contributions, which are generally deductible from income by the taxpayer.[16] Some refer to this as an effective matching grant system for private charities and the other non-profit organizations specified by the Code. They are also favored with special postal rates if they qualify.[17]

Considerable controversy surrounds these special tax treatments. Applying originally to just a few church and charitable organizations, special tax treatment has snowballed to now include education, scientific, literary, public safety, cruelty prevention, hospital service, amateur sport, social welfare, business, labor, agricultural, horticultural, insurance and a host of other types of organizations.

The rationale for exempt status is very specific for some organizations, and can be determined from the records of the congressional debate surrounding the enactment of their exempt status. But the overall rationale for exempt status and the deductibility of contributions, which are separate issues, is more fluid and subject to debate.

Many fear that the elimination of this special tax status would truly lead to a reduction in private giving. This assumes that taxpayers contribute only so that they can deduct. Some, on the other hand, believe that the haphazard tax expenditure approach to the encouragement of socially beneficial behavior is wasteful. Direct, controllable, selective grants to charity by government might be more efficient. This position, of course, raises the question of government control and becomes, at least for religious organizations, a constitutional issue on the separation of church and state.

The notion of encouraging creativity, experimentation, personal and community involvement is behind the strongest present rationale for exempt status and deductibility. At the very beginning of the American experiment, the astute Alexis de Tocqueville observed the important value of these organizations both to fostering a sense of community and to serving as a competing source of public benefit to assure that government does not dominate our national life. The aspect of the tax code under discussion here helps to reflect this.

As one tax expenditure among many, however, there is much to criticize about the deductibility of charitable giving. (1) Since it is a tax expenditure, it is clear that the government participates in private giving to the extent of a percentage of the taxpayer's gift that corresponds to the taxpayer's effective tax rate. (2) As a matching grant, it is inequitably skewed to favor those with higher rates. (3) Given some recent abuses by groups that are "religious" for tax purposes only, it is also becoming more and more difficult to define a religious organization and to distinguish religious activity from business and political activity. First Amendment freedoms make IRS intrusions into these distinctions very dangerous from a civil liberties' viewpoint. (4) It is being gradually eroded by the increasing standard deduction. This upward adjustment, which has recently been indexed, has limited substantially the number of those who itemize deductions, thus defeating the purpose of the deduction.

There seems to be very little political support for eliminating these exemptions, though a number of proposals for reform are being discussed.

The necessity of the tax exempt status for churches is open for question. Their internal operations probably should be exempt under current tax theory since contributions to their upkeep by members for the mutual benefit of members are not really "taxable events," like earning income or appreciation on investments. However, from a tax perspective, the separate question of their charitable and humanitarian activities is not really a religious question, but a secular and political one. As with other such organizations, religious or not, should our national policy favor their existence and growth? If so, should it use the tax system to accomplish this policy?

A corollary question is whether the overall fairness problem created by allowing tax expenditures is outweighed, in this case, by the policy benefits of using the tax code to encourage pluralism, experimentation, creativity, and charitable giving.

---

[1]Robert Kuttner, *Revolt of the Haves: Tax Rebellions and Hard Times* (New York: Simon & Schuster, 1980), p. 250. Technically, the phrase "seems to mean net investment in manufacturing plant and equipment" (p. 251). However, in most political debate, it appears to conform to the definition given in the text.

[2]Nota, p. 71.

[3]Bob Kuttner, "Savings, Investment, and Distribution: Lessons from Abroad on Capital Formation," *Growth with Fairness: Progressive Economic Policies for the Eighties,* Robert S. McIntyre, ed. (Washington, D.C.: Institute on Taxation and Economic Policy, 1983), p. 10.

[4]Kuttner, "Savings, Investment, and Distribution. . .", p. 10.

[5]Kuttner, *Revolt of the Haves,* p. 254f.

[6]Kuttner, *Revolt of the Haves,* p. 269.

[7]Joint Committee on Taxation, *Tax Policy and Capital Formation* (Washington, D.C.: Government Printing Office, 1977), pp. 18-19.

[8]See Ronald D. Pasquariello, Donald W. Shriver, Jr. and Alan Geyer, *Redeeming the City: Theology, Politics and Urban Policy* (New York: Pilgrim Press, 1982), p. 74.

[9]See Brandon, *et. al.,* pp. 44-47 for many reasons similar to those expressed here.

[10]Quoted in McIntyre and Folen, p. 8.

[11]Federal Reserve Board of Governors, *Public Policy and Capital Formation* (Washington, D.C., 1981), p. 7.

[12]Stanley S. Surrey, *Pathways to Tax Reform: The Concept of Tax Expenditures* (Cambridge: Harvard University Press, 1973), p. 131.

[13]Surrey, p. 136. Surrey is using 1972 figures for these examples.

[14]Joint Economic Committee, *Annual Report* (Washington, D.C.: U.S. Government Printing Office, 1982), p. 37.

[15]Title 26, section 501c of the Internal Revenue Code.

[16]Title 26, section 170 of the Internal Revenue Code.

[17]39 Code of Federal Regulations, Parts 132, 134.

*Tax reform means don't tax you, don't tax me
tax the fellow behind the tree.*

Senator Russell B. Long

Chapter 10:
Evaluating the Major Tax
Reform Proposals
(On the Fairness of Some Proposed Tax Changes)

Programs for tax reform, like snowflakes, are multitudinous, and each slightly different from the other. There were, for example, twelve different flat tax proposals on the legislative agenda in 1982, and numerous other touted in the literature on the subject. Sometimes they are as artfully constructed as snowflakes such that only careful examination will uncover the hidden intricacies.

This chapter examines only some of the major proposals and tests them against the criteria listed in Chapter 4. The purpose of this survey is to inform the reader about some of the possibilities of tax reform, and to demonstrate how they can be evaluated.[1] The criteria have to do with these factors: comprehensivity (taxing all income), progressivity (taxing according to ability-to-pay), redistribution of the tax burden, simplicity and efficiency.

Broadening the Tax Base

Former Senator Floyd Haskell likes to tell this story. When he had the first meeting of his newly organized Taxpayers Committee, sitting around the oval table before him were former IRS Commissioners and Assistant Secretaries of the Treasury and other offices from all of the recent presidential administrations. They represented every political persuasion from conservative to liberal. Anxiety swept over the Senator. How, he thought, was he to get these folks to agree on what needs to be done. He projected months of work on concensus. A few hours into their first meeting, however, they all agreed that the driving need was to broaden the base.

Though the battle starts when one gets down to details, broadening the base—i.e., the amount and types of income that are subject to taxation—is the one tax reform issue that liberals, conservatives and everyone in between agrees on. A more accurate name for this reform proposal would be restoring the tax base, because it does not mean so much adding new elements to the tax base as it would entail repeal of all or nearly all congressionally installed, and often presidentially cajoled, tax breaks: deductions, credits, exclusions and exemptions. It is sometimes called comprehensive income taxation.

The political appeal of broadening the base is that it calls for the repeal of all of the distorting aspects of the tax system. The political problem is that it would eliminate everyone's favorite tax break. Included would be deductions for charitable contributions, medical expenses, home mortgage interest rates; exemptions from tax on social security and AFDC, fringe benefits; the capital gains exclusion.[2] They and many more, would all go.

The American public is ambivalent when it comes down to the details of tax reform. In a recent Harris poll, 62 percent of the public backed a flat-rate tax with few deductions. However, when asked about individual deductions, the same people overwhelmingly opposed their repeal. 80 percent favored retaining the deduction for medical expenses, 71 percent the home mortgage interest deduction, and so on.[3]

Besides the fact that every exemption has a well-formed constituency to protect it, this is a more serious concern: Many persons and institutions feel dependent on these exemptions for their financial well-being. Taxing the social security benefits of the elderly poor, for example, could totally shatter their fragile hold on the basic necessities. Elimination of the home mortgage interest deduction could force many homeowners into fore-closure. There are, however, ways of protecting these people in the transition, and thoughtful base broadening proposals have included them: by increasing benefits to the poor, or preserving the home mortgage interest deduction with a cap to target it to moderate income households, and so forth.

From the perspective of the criteria laid out here, broadening or restoring the base by the elimination of all tax expenditures, with the inclusion of carefully thought out transitional steps, is the best means for achieving an equitable and progressive income tax rate. It would conform to the five criteria articulated earlier, and would be an important first step in dealing with the knotty problem of the distribution of wealth.

1. Comprehensivity. All the base broadening proposals favor adopting a relatively comprehensive definition of income as the primary basis for taxation.

2. Progressivity. Base broadening proposals are of two minds concerning tax rates. Some favor maintaining graduated rates, while others seek a flat rate. Only the graduated rate proposals meet the requirement of progressivity.[4] Moreover, with a broader base the progressive rates would be lower than under the present system.

3. Simplicity. The tax code would be considerably simpler because there would be no exemptions, no capital gains exclusions, no possibility for tax shelters (and a great deal of unemployment among tax lawyers).

4. Efficiency. Efficiency would be increased because investment and work decisions would be influenced less by tax considerations.

5. Redistribution. Redistribution will be affected somewhat in that taxes will rise for those who now make heavy use of tax preferences and fall for those who do not. However, the amount of redistribution would be limited because the proposals deal with income and not the accumulation of wealth.

Reducing Rates

Every taxpayer feels that his/her tax bracket is too high. Whether it is or is not depends on what it pays for. Broadening the base circumvents that discussion somewhat because, since it would increase revenues, tax rates could be reduced substantially and still yield at least the same revenue. Many taxpayers, especially those in the lower brackets, pay artificially higher rates on their income. Narrowing the tax base by increasing the number of exemptions over the years has led to higher rates. The higher rates were needed to raise the total desired amount of revenue.

Rate reducing proposals vary from (1) maintaining the present rate graduations at lower percentages, through (2) reducing the number of brackets considerably, (3) to establishing a single flat rate.

While appealing, the flat rate ultimately fails the test of fairness. Though proposals for it have been around for quite a while, the flat rate concept has recently enjoyed a place in the sun because President Reagan pronounced it "very tempting" in 1982, his Treasury Secretary called it the fairest tax of all, David Stockman promised to inject it with life in the President's 1984 budget proposal (a promise he fortunately found he could not keep) and the Treasury Department offered a "modified flat tax" reform proposal to the public in December of 1984.

The proposals take two basic forms: either one flat rate, or a three or four step flat rate (this latter approaching simplified graduated rate proposals). Either form may come with or without exemptions, depending on the ideology of the architect of the plan.

The one rate flat-taxers usually propose a figure around 20 percent,[5] which means that all taxpayers would pay twenty percent of their taxable income. Other proposals include flat rate scales of 10, 15, and 20 percent, or some similar, simple graduated scale.[6]

The Joint Committee on Taxation has calculated that a flat rate of about 12 percent would raise the same amount of revenue in 1984 as the current income tax if the tax base were broadened to eliminate all tax expenditures. Without tax broadening, a flat rate of about 18.5 percent would be needed.[7] Those individuals who currently pay rates above these figures would get a tax break, those who currently pay less would receive a tax increase.

The bottom line on the one rate flat tax proposal is that it is not fair. Consider Mr. Ashley and Mr. Bentley. Suppose Mr. Bentley has a family of four to support, and earned $15,000 per year and Mr. Ashley, in similar circumstances, earned $150,000 per year. The cost of living impacts each of these families differently. All of Mr. B's salary is going to support his family. A large part of Mr. A's income goes towards the emollients of the good life. In what sense is it fair to leave Mr. B with $12,000 to support his family, amd Mr. A with upwards of $120,000?

The one rate proposal is also unfair because it does not affect the distribution of wealth. If everyone is required to pay 20 percent of their taxable income, than the before-tax and after-tax distribution of wealth is the same. Everyone just has twenty percent less accrued income.

About the flat rate proposals with variable rates—or "modified flat rates"—well, all right, but why? How do they differ from a graduated income tax, which has the advantage of being more progressive? Besides, a flat rate, modified to include two or more rates is no longer flat.

Reductions in the graduated income rates meet our criteria. Flat tax proposals do not. Here is why.

1. Comprehensivity. Some rate reduction proposals, be they graduated or flat, are comprehensive, others are not. Those that have a broad definition of income would meet at least this criterion.

2. Progressivity. Most flat rate proposals would not correct the present injustices in the system. Higher income persons would not pay a greater share of their income than those below them. Rather they would pay the same share. Taxes for people in the top brackets would be lowered, and for those in the lower brackets would be raised. Graduated income rate reduction proposals move in the direction of this criterion, though they should also have to meet the standard of vertical equity.

3. Simplicity. The complexity of our present system stems from the tax loopholes or expenditures. The simplicity of flat rate systems would be a function of the number of loopholes they allow or eliminate. Tax forms would be reduced to one page, tax lawyers and accounts made superfluous. Inflation-caused bracket creep would become irrelevant since there would be virtually no brackets, and tax manipulation would be unnecessary. But the loss of progressivity would be too high a price to pay for this kind of simplicity, when a progressive tax with a graduated scale and no exemptions would be just as simple.

4. Efficiency. This would be improved because taxes would not be used as economic incentives. With graduated flat-rate systems, however, workers would still have to fear getting pushed up into higher tax brackets.

5. Redistribution. Flat tax rates are not redistributive. The one rate flat tax does not alter the distribution of income or wealth, while the variable flat rate proposals require a lowering of the average tax rates paid by the wealthy and raising the rates paid the lower classes.[8] Reduced graduated rates, on the other hand, would allow for some redistribution but, as pointed out before, it is a question of some debate whether the amount of redistribution possible within these parameters is sufficient to meet biblical standards.

Taxing Consumption Instead of Income

This alternative has been taken seriously by a number of tax policy analysts, and may be subject to quite a bit of debate in the future. Consumption taxation does not meet the criteria set out in this book.

A person has two basic choices with regard to income: it can be saved or it can be spent. Consumption taxes would simply tax that portion of income that is spent or consumed, and leave savings untouched. Taxpayers would report all salaries, wages, dividends, interest, rental income and proceeds of sales or assets. They would subtract net additions to savings: deposits to savings accounts, purchases of stocks, bonds and other income-producing assets.[9]

That is the heart of the system. Potentially it could be fraught with all the inequities and problems of the present system because it is merely a tax on that portion of income that is spent. It could look like the current income system, i.e., have graduated rates with various exemptions, or no exemptions, or flat rates, or what have you. Much would depend on the extent Congress enacted any of these special provisions.

Here is a simplified example of how it could operate. Suppose Mr. Bentley, with $30,000 in income in 1984, bought $3,000 in stock, put $250 in savings, and withdrew $1,000 from his checking account. The $3,000 and the $250 would be classified as savings. The $1,000 would be called an expenditure. He would be taxed on $27,750, less any exemptions that might be allowable.

Consumption taxation would make saving a tax shelter. People would be encouraged to save because anything so tucked away would be beyond the reach of the IRS. The more frugal a person would be, the less his/her tax bite would be. More savings would mean more money available for investment without the distortions of the present system of tax incentives.

When it is subjected to our five criteria, consumption taxation does not stand up well. This is because consumption taxes are really sales taxes by another name. Sales taxes are, after all, taxes we pay on what we spend.

1. Comprehensivity. A lot here would depend on what form the system takes. Without exemptions, it could touch consumption comprehensively. It would not have the same effect on income. In fact, the higher one's income, the less of it that would be taxed. Low income persons simply cannot save any portion of their income and, without exemptions, what they earn would be taxed at extremely high rates. High income persons could shelter a great deal of their earnings in various savings mechanisms. Consumption taxation could not tax income comprehensively.

2. Progressivity. This too would depend on the final shape of the system. Any statutory degree of progressivity in the rate scale is possible. But this progressivity would be nominal. Since the system itself would tax only consumption, it would impact more severely on low income persons who consume all their income and are unable to shelter it in savings.

3. Efficiency. Efficiency would be improved since the tax would not negatively influence the decision to save, that is, it would not fall more heavily on some kinds of savings than others. There would therefore be no incentives to favor one type of savings or investment over another.

4. Simplicity. While there would be a decrease in some of the technical aspects of reporting taxes, consumption tax systems have been considered complicated (in their pure forms) even by their advocates. In addition, compliance could worsen as taxpayers give into the temptation not to report sales of assets.

5. Redistribution. Under a consumption system, persons who could and did save a large portion of their incomes would pay less than under an

income tax. It would be easier to amass large fortunes. Most consumption tax advocates realize this potential for putting huge amounts of wealth in the hands of a few persons. Many of them propose a substantial tax on gifts and bequests to offset this possibility.[10] However, against the consumption tax is still the argument that economic capacity is determined by income, not consumption. Income represents the power to consume or save, and therefore it represents control of economic resources. Furthermore, the accumulation of wealth not only increases the power to consume, but confers social power, influence, security and access to numerous social opportunities that would not be available to those without this wealth.[11]

A Miscellany of Other Tax Reform Proposals

The American tax system is so distorted that it has stimulated numerous tax reform proposals. Of course they cannot all be discussed here. For the remainder of this chapter. we would like to highlight some along with their most important features.

1. Indexing.

Indexing the tax system means building in an automatic adjustment for inflation. Inflation stimulates bracket creep and causes capital income to be overstated. Indexing proposals would compensate for both of these effects of inflation.

Indexing became a part of the federal income tax during the Reagan Administration, to take effect in 1985. Some strong voices have been heard in favor of its repeal, as one way of dealing with the large budget deficits expected in that year and those following. Repeal, for them, is a favored alternative because no other proposals to reduce the deficits seem to be politically viable.

Indexing would improve equity since real income and not imputed income would be taxed,[12] but it would have no effect on efficiency since the tax system would continue to distort the allocation of resources among investments. It would also complicate the administration of taxes which would now have to be indexed to include the impact of inflation. As a way of compensating for the effects of inflation, indexing makes sense. But it should be put in place as an overall scheme of tax reform proposals that would mitigate other inequities in the system.

2. Taxing Corporations

The corporation tax has declined drastically over the years. Advocates of eliminating it have made two claims about its inappropriateness: that it represents a double taxation on the corporate owners (stockholders), and that it is detrimental to productivity. As pointed out in earlier chapters, neither of these arguments are convincing. In the first place, corporate taxes were highest in the period when this country was most productive. Secondly, lacking a corporate tax, the income of the stockholder could become sheltered in the form of increased value of the stock until the stockholder decides to sell it, when it would be taxed at lower, capital gains rates.

The goal of the corporate taxation should be, as the 1984 Treasury Department tax proposals recommended, a simplified corporate tax structure that eliminates all forms of tax incentives that lead to gross misallocations of investment. As a matter of fairness, the tax should be no less than the marginal income tax rate on average wage-earners.[13]

3. Social Security Taxes

The bipartisan National Commission on Social Security Reform made a number of sensible proposals to salvage the social security system,[14] but none of the proposals managed to squeeze the regressivity out of that system. The way it works now, social security taxes the lower and middle-income groups heavily to support the retired population.

Various progressive reforms have been proposed: removal of the ceiling on wages subject to tax, personal exemptions based on family size, joint returns. The obvious first step demanded by fairness is to remove the ceiling on wages. However, even more equity would be achieved if the tax were levied on all income with exemptions based on family size, rather than limiting it to earned income.[15] While this would complicate the system somewhat, the sacrifice in simplicity would be worth the achievement in equity.

---

[1]Further information on any of these, and many others, can be had from the organizations mentioned in the appendix.

[2]For a detailed summary of the proposal, see *Analysis of Proposals Relating to Broadening the Base and Lowering the Rates of the Income Tax,* U.S. Congress, Joint Committee on Taxation (Washington, D.C.: Government Printing Office, 1982).

[3]*Business Week* (September 6, 1982), p. 15.

[4]Flat rate proposals will be discussed later in this chapter. The tax rate structure is independent of the type of base it is imposed on.

[5]The Kemp-Kasten bill has a single rate of 25%.

[6]The Treasury Tax Reform Proposal (1984) has a "modified" flat rate scale of 15%, 25%, and 35%; Bradley-Gaphardt has rates of 14%, 26% and 30%.

[7]*Revising the Individual Income Tax* (Washington, D.C.: Congressional Budget Office, 1983), p. 52.

[8]See Pamela Fessler, "Flat-Rate Tax Plan Advanced as Radical Cure for Problems of Existing Revenue System," *Congressional Quarterly Weekly* (June 5, 1982), pp. 1332-1333.

[9]*Revising the Individual Income Tax,* p. 111.

[10]See, for example, Paul N. Courant and Edward M. Gramlich, "Taxing What We Spend, Not What We Earn," *The Washington Post,* (June 12, 1983), p. B8. The authors give some arguments in favor of the consumption tax, most of which have been refuted here.

[11]Galper, "Tax Policy," p. 189.

[12]See Galper, "Tax Policy," p. 193.

[13]Citizens for Tax Justice, "The Reagan Tax Shift, Part IV, Where Do We Go from Here?", in *Tax Policy Guide,* no. 2 (June, 1982), p. 8.

[14]Among the proposals were these: accelerated scheduled rate increases, a one time delay in cost of living adjustments, coverage for employees of nonprofit institutions and new federal employees, and taxation of one-half of social security benefits for recipients above $20,000 (individuals) and $25,000 (couples).

[15]Nancy Teeters, "Payroll Tax" in Richard A. Musgrave, Ed., *Broadbased Taxes: New Options and Sources* (Baltimore: The John Hopkins University Press, 1973), pp. 110-111.

In sooth, the sorrow of such days
Is not to be express'd,
When he that takes and he that pays
Are both alike distress'd.

William Cowper

Chapter 11:
Tips for Tax Reformers

Tax reform will be a key issue for the rest of the decade—and beyond—if the nation really intends to do something about the jungle of injustices that are now built into the system. But it is the projected deficits of $200 to $300 billion that will really keep tax reform on the front burner. The degree to which the present system can be manipulated to meet the challenge of those deficits is limited.

There are tax-reform proposals on every desk on Capitol Hill. A missing ingredient in all of them has been the participation of the American people in their development. Most tax-reform proposals come out of well-endowed, partisan think tanks and are advocated by highly paid corporate lobbyists who work to adjust the system in the direction of their special interests.

Although the American people are increasingly discontent with the tax system, many things keep them from trying to reform it. One of the major factors seems to be their perception that the system is too complex for them to understand. The system is indeed complex—necessarily so. However, one need not have mastered all of its complexities to bring about change, just as one need not know everything about the inner workings of an automobile to know that there is something wrong, to get intelligent advice, and to correct the problem.

There are a few simple principles which the average American can use to make judgments about the equity of the present system, and about proposals for reform.[1]

1. *Any tax deduction benefits those with high incomes more than those with low.* Deductions are used only by people who itemize their taxes—approximately 30 to 35 percent of all taxpayers, who tend to be in the

upper income brackets. Furthermore, a dollar of deduction saves the high-bracket (50 percent) taxpayer 50 cents, but saves a low-bracket taxpayer as little as 11 cents.

2. *No tax incentive or deduction is free.* They cost the government—and eventually the taxpayer—money, just as any outlay for government programs does. Only the form of the payment differs. Tax deductions, incentives, credits and exemptions now amount to 40 percent of the federal budget, and are climbing.

3. *Tax exemptions for some mean higher taxes for others.* The government must raise revenue to cover the costs of its operations and the programs that are required to meet our national needs. If it exempts some people from the normal tax structure, then it must raise the tax rates of everyone else in order to meet its financial obligations. It is estimated that taxes could be lowered by one third just by eliminating all tax expenditures.

4. *Anything that sounds like a sales tax is regressive.* Such taxes are regressive because the poor and members of the middle class must use a higher percentage of their incomes in acquiring the goods and services taxed. Sales taxes are also regressive because they tax the basic items which are a larger part of lower-income budgets. Value-added taxes and consumption taxes fall into this category, and are therefore highly undesirable.

5. *Social security taxes are regressive.* Such taxes are levied only on wage income and not on income from wealth and capital. They are flat taxes on wages and salaries up to a certain maximum. Any raises in social security taxes, therefore, are regressive because such taxes take a greater proportion from lower than from higher wage earners, and leave largely untaxed those whose income is primarily from wealth rather than from wages.

6. *Deductions, credits and exemptions add to the complexity of the system.* Each one of these represents one more factor that must be added, subtracted, multiplied or divided in calculating one's yearly taxes. They have increased the complexity of the system so much that the IRS commissioner recently admitted that some tax returns are too involved for his team to audit. They have also given rise to a new cottage industry—tax lawyers who put all of their creative energies into figuring out ways to take advantage of the tax system for their clients.

7. *Tax shelters are paid for by taxpayers who do not invest in them.* A tax shelter is more than a typical deduction. It is an accounting procedure

whereby the investor gets a two-to-one or four-to-one return on his or her investment in the form of tax savings rather than of income produced by the investment. A person who invested $10,000 in a llama farm might, if it is a well-organized shelter, get as much as $20,000 to $40,000 in tax deductions. The rest of the American taxpayers would get no benefit from the farm but would have to pay for these deductions through higher taxes of their own.

8. *Flattening tax rates means wringing the progressivity out of the system.* Many of the flat tax bills now before Congress propose doing away with all or almost all tax deductions, which would reduce our tax forms to postcard size. Despite this advantage, however, the flat rate is not progressive. It would reduce taxes for families earning more than $30,000 to $50,000 (depending on which rate is used). But all families earning less than that—more than half of the families in our country—would experience a tax increase. Simplicity need not be bought at the price of reduced progressivity. Tax expenditures, not the progressive scale, cause most of the system's complexity.

9. *Across-the-board adjustments in rates do little to solve our tax problems.* Everyone knows now that the across-the-board cuts in personal taxes made by the Reagan administration benefited the rich. This year, those lucky Americans who make more than $200,000 can expect a tax break 33 times greater than that of the average worker. As these disparities suggest, the main problem with across-the-board cuts is that they do nothing to compensate for the injustices in the system. The higher-income taxpayer continues to reap greater advantages than the less affluent.

10. *Estate and gift taxes are progressive.* Because only persons of means have sizable estates to transfer, estate and gift taxes usually affect high-income persons only. Of the 200,747 estate tax returns filed in 1976, 75 percent were for estates of $100,000 or more. Most tax theorists believe that estate taxes are fair. Yet estate and gift taxes have been all but eliminated by current tax policies. Only the wealthiest 0.3 percent of all those who die in any one year are subject to federal estate or gift taxes. Wealth is a source of economic power, social status and, hence, political influence. If equality of control over society's priorities is a major concern in a democracy, then estate and gift taxes are two of the easiest ways to ensure that equality. They make the transfer of great accumulations of wealth between generations difficult.

In our view the first, necessary step in tax reform is to broaden the base. This meets our criteria, and seem politically viable. But is it sufficient?

There is no easy answer to that question, yet it one that Christians must not only face, but must also make part of the public dialogue. And why must they raise that question? Because they are concerned about ending poverty, not just out of expediency, but out of a sense of mission that stems directly from the biblical concern for the poor. The ethical challenge for them is to reduce poverty and narrow the gap between poor and non-poor.

Our present tax base is income, which consists essentially of wages and salaries, with some inclusion of income from capital. Base broadening proposals bypass the question of the adequacy of this base. They would increase that base to include all income from capital. In our view, there is not enough taxable income, as officially defined or as proposed by the base broadeners, to meet the biblical standards for equity. To meet these standards, the tax system must also reach wealth.

Discussions of redistribution have centered on income rather than wealth. Many of the financial returns from wealth are not counted as income. An outstanding example is unrealized capital gains, which are computed as part of a person's wealth, which give a person access to status and power, but which are not taxed until they are realized. They then are either taxed at a lower rate than ordinary income, or are offset by losses that are often paper transactions.

American attitudes are peculiarly ambivalent when it comes to taxing wealth. We easily recommend it for underdeveloped countries, where land is wealth, under the guise of land reform. Yet we resist any attempt to tax wealth here. This ambivalence shows up in the two forms of wealth taxation that are on our books: estate and gift taxes, and the property tax.

Bequests and gifts are ways of passing wealth down between generations, and preserving concentrations of wealth. A strong case can be made for taxing such bequests, on the basis that the inheritor did nothing to merit the wealth, except to be born into the right family at the right time. It cannot be claimed that the bequest accrues to the inheritor from natural talent or from hard work. It is simply the luck of the draw. Yet, estate and gift taxes have only amounted to about 2 percent of federal budget receipts.[2] Property taxes are also a tax on wealth. They have been the debatable focus of tax revolts in recent years, which have lead to the mitigation of this form of tax.

Other advanced industrial countries (Austria, Denmark, Finland, Ireland, the Netherlands, Norway, Sweden and West Germany) have managed to put an annual tax on wealth in place. It is a tax on the value of assets less the liabilities of the individual or households.[3] Why have we not been able to follow suit? The most repeated answer has to do with the fluidity of economic class lines in this country. Americans believe that improved economic and social status is easily available to them through hard work and savings. The facts, of course, belie this belief. Savings hardly produce wealth. There is realtively little fluidity between classes. Wealth statistics remain the same over the years. Concentrations of wealth are preserved through inheritance. The accumulation of wealth is due as much to luck—being in the right place at the right time—as to talent, since there are an unnumbered quantity of talented losers in the wealth game.

No one can say with certainty what a fair distribution of wealth would be. Nor do we know the right way to achieve it. But taxing wealth is technically possible. The next task is to make it politically viable. The narrowing of the gap between the rich and the poor will probably take the form of gradual change based upon public dialogue and astute legislative action. Christians need to initiate the dialogue and stimulate the action. It is not being dealt with otherwise within our society.

---

[1] The author is grateful to *The Christian Century* for permission to reprint (with revisions) "Tips for Tax Reformers," 101 (1984), 542-543.

[2] 2.6% was the post-World War II high in 1972.

[3] Joseph Pechman, *Federal Tax Policy,* pp. 242-43.

Appendix:
Ways and Means in Tax Reform

Groups of all kinds, from high-powered pressure groups to low-key research groups, have focussed some of their attention on tax policy over the years. Things have changed recently. New groups, devoted entirely to tax policy issues, and increases in staff-size of the older groups have been the order of the day. These changes have no doubt been stimulated by the increasing malleability of the tax system to the peculiar needs of special interests, and in particular to congressional legislation that has opened the door to tax loopholes.

The relatively short list that follows covers most of the tax organizations that are focussed on federal tax reform. The intention of the listing is to give the reader a sense of the kinds of organizations which are now active in tax policy, and to lay out some resources for those who wish to dig more deeply in the area.

A 1981 survey, which claimed to be comprehensive, listed only 26 organizations exclusively devoted to change on the federal income level.[1] Business-oriented groups are the most numerous. Their interests are increased capital formation, greater productivity and more rapid depreciation. Among these would be the American Council for Capital Formation, the Tax Foundation, the Heritage Foundation, the Taxpayer's Foundation.

The public at large is ill-organized. The public seems to become concerned usually only when affected by changes in tax policy, particularly revenue raises. Public interest groups are woefully under-represented and under-resourced. In this group would fall The Taxpayers Committee, Citizens for Tax Justice, and Public Citizen's Tax Reform Research Group. These groups take a broad approach to reform of the system in general rather than focussing on particular aspects of the tax system.

Think tank types, such as Brookings (ideologically liberal or moderate) and the American Enterprise Institute (ideologically conservative), form a third grouping. In the remaining, disparate group are the balance-the-budget organizations (such as the National Tax Limitation Committee), and taxpayer watchdogs against IRS abuse (the National Tax Equality Association).

Conspicuously absent are groups which devote much of their energy to lobbying for social programs on the outlay side of the budget. They seem to have left tax policy to groups who want to lower taxes, or distort the system for the benefit of their special interests.

American Council for Capital Formation
1850 K St., N.W., Suite 520
Washington, D.C. 20006
202/293-5811

Advocates legislation to encourage savings and investment and to reduce capital gains tax. Publishes *Newswatch* monthly ($50/year), along with "Action Bulletins" to assist in lobbying.

American Enterprise Institute for Public Policy Research
Tax Policy Studies Division
1150 17th St., N.W.
Washington, D.C. 20036
202/862-5800

Analyzes and educates about the impact of taxation on economic behavior. Publishes *Public Opinion* bimonthly ($26/year). Recent tax publications: *The Tax Treatment of Social Security* and *Taxing the Income from U.S. Corporation Investments Abroad.*

The Brookings Institution
Economic Studies Program
1775 Massachusetts Ave., N.W.
Washington, D.C. 20036
202/797-6110

In the course of its broad-based research on domestic and international economic issues, it researches current issues in taxation like comprehensive income taxation, inflation and taxes, tax expenditures, etc. It publishes *The Brookings Papers on Economic Activity* twice a year. Recent tax publications: *The Economics of Taxation* and *How Taxes Affect Economic Behavior.*

The Heritage Foundation
214 Massachusetts Avenue, N.E.
Washington, D.C. 20002
202/546-4400

In the course of researching social, environmental, energy and economic issues, it occasionally analyzes tax issues in *Policy Review,* published quarterly ($15/year). Recent tax publications: *Taxes and Philanthrophy— The Need for Action* and *Congress and the Budget.*

National Council for a World Peace Tax Fund
2121 Decatur Place, N.W.
Washington, D.C. 20008
202/483-3751

Supports legislation to provide that a taxpayer morally opposed to war may elect to have his/her income and estate and gift tax payments spent on non-military projects through a government trust—the World Peace Tax Fund.

National Taxpayers Legal Fund
122 C St., N.W.
Washington, D.C. 20001
202/638-1404

Concerned with government waste of tax dollars in all facets of the budget and the investigative abuses of IRS employees. Organizes the Legal Fund, a non-profit public interest advocacy group, compiles a referral list of attorneys who are willing to take citizen tax cases.

National Tax Limitation Committee
500 N. Washington St.
Falls Church, VA 20046
703/534-2500

Supports state and federal constitutional amendments to limit government spending to the level of economic growth. Publishes *Inside Report,* a newsletter of Federal and State lobbying efforts on the issue.

National Taxpayers Union
713 Maryland Ave., N.E.
Washington, D.C. 20005
202/543-1300

Seeks to implement a Balance the Budget Amendment and to reduce government spending and taxes. Assists state taxpayer groups with tax reduction and limitation initiatives. Publishes *Dollars and Sense,* a monthly newsletter ($15/year), and an annual voting survey on congressional spending attitudes.

Public Citizen's Tax Reform Research Group
215 Pennsylvania Ave., S.E.
Washington, D.C. 20003
202/546-4996

Concerned about an equitable tax policy; supports preservation of corporate income tax, lower tax rates and elimination of tax subsidies, believing that the code should only raise revenue. Publishes *People and Taxes* monthly ($12.50/year).

Tax Foundation, Inc.
1 Thomas Circle, N.W.
Suite 500
Washington, D.C. 20005
202/822-9050

Advocates reduction of tax obstacles to capital formation. Publishes *Facts and Figures on Government Finance* every two years; and *Fiscal Policy Forum, Monthly Tax Features,* and *Tax Review* ($50/year for all three).

Taxpayers Committee
133 North Carolina Ave., S.E.
Washington, D.C. 20003
202/546-2442

Advocates simplifying and revising the tax code so that it is fair and truly progressive. Its chief goal is education of the American public about the need for tax reform and the importance of their participation in tax reform. Conducts lectures and seminars.

Taxpayers' Foundation
317 C St., N.E.
Washington, D.C. 20003
202/543-3070

Publishes *More for Less,* a "how-to" manual for implementing productivity and economic efficiency in local government spending, and *Fiscal Watchdog,* a monthly municipal cost cutting report.

Government Organizations

Internal Revenue Service
1111 Constitution Ave., N.W.
Washington, D.C. 20224
202/566-4115

Administers and enforces internal revenue laws. Provides information and guidance on tax matters, including assistance in the preparation of tax returns. Provides data on national income and taxes. Publishes annual reports.

Office of Assistant Secretary for Tax Policy
Main Treasury Building
Washington, D.C. 20220
202/566-5561

Formulates and executes tax policies and programs. Develops and provides economic analysis of legislation.

Office of Management and Budget
Executive Office Building
17th Street and Pennsylvania Ave., N.W.
Washington, D.C. 00000
202/395-3000

Assists the President in the preparation and formulation of the budget; informs the President of needed adjustments in tax rates and tax policies.

Congressional Budget Office
Second and D Streets, S.W.
Washington, D.C. 20515
202/226-2700

Prepares budget and tax data and analyzes alternative fiscal policies to aid Congress in its decision making. Publishes valuable annual reports on tax expenditures.

House Ways and Means Committee
The United States House of Representatives
Washington, D.C. 20515
202/224-3625

Has jurisdiction over tax legislation.

Joint Committee on Taxation
The United States House of Representatives
Washington, D.C. 20515
202/225-3621

Provides technical staff support for House Ways and Means and Senate Finance Committee. Authors informative studies of various aspects of tax policy.

Senate Finance Committee
The United States Senate
Washington, D.C. 20510
202/224-4515

Has jurisdiction over tax legislation.